HOW TO
PRAY
POWERFULLY

A GUIDE TO
50 BIBLE PRAYERS
FOR MEN

DAVID MCLAUGHLAN

BARBOUR

PUBLISHING

Print ISBN 978-1-63609-561-5

Previously published as *Prayer That Has the Power to Change Your Life.*

Published by Barbour Publishing, Inc., 1810 Barbour Drive, Uhrichsville, Ohio 44683, www.barbourbooks.com

Our mission is to inspire the world with the life-changing message of the Bible.

Member of the
Evangelical Christian
Publishers Association

Printed in China.

INTRODUCTION

Who prays? And why?

Humanity prays—or the vast majority of us do, and always have.

People pray to the one true God, false deities, the universe, wise men, or Mother Earth. People have prayed to the sun, various animals, and imaginary monsters. Even some atheists, who would normally have no time for a deity, will pray in times of need.

All around the world, in many different ways, and for countless generations, humanity has prayed.

The Bible tells us that as long as there have been people there has been prayer of one sort or another. But where's the proof?

Recent archeological findings suggest that the first stone buildings may have been created as places of worship. Who was worshipping and who was being worshipped they can't say. But it seems that for as long as there has been "community" in the world, there has been worship and prayer.

So, why?

People have always possessed a great need to speak to something or someone beyond their understanding. Why that would be such an essential part of being human is difficult to imagine without considering the existence of a Creator God.

But the practice would have been discarded long ago (along with living in caves and hunting wooly mammoths) if it was a one-sided conversation—if there were no answers.

The fact that so many of us still pray says something. It says that prayers are answered and that even now they are changing lives.

Prayer runs like a brightly colored thread through the Bible. The people in it who talked to, accepted the will of, and even argued with the Almighty were as varied a group as you would find anywhere. And prayer changed each of their lives.

Let's take a look at how that happened, why it happened, and how we can put what they learned to good use in our lives today.

1

"I'VE DONE WHAT I CAN, LORD. TAKE ME HOME."

A Prayer of Thanks for a Life of Devotion

Then took he him up in his arms, and blessed God, and said, Lord, now lettest thou thy servant depart in peace, according to thy word: for mine eyes have seen thy salvation, which thou hast prepared before the face of all people; a light to lighten the Gentiles, and the glory of thy people Israel.

LUKE 2:28–32 KJV

Simeon is described as a "just and devout" (Luke 2:25) person, a description that hardly stands out in the Bible, but in Jerusalem under Roman occupation, that would have been a tough row to hoe, just as it is now.

In seeking the "consolation of Israel" (Luke 2:25), he was doing what many are still doing today and praying God would take a hand in the country's future direction. At some point in his life he had been assured this would really happen. So he waited, and waited, and waited.

As he watched the depravity of Israel's Jewish rulers and the brutality of her Roman occupiers, he must have despaired. He was growing old, and things seemed worse than ever.

But on this particular day, the Holy Spirit seems to have done its version of coughing to attract his attention and jerking a thumb toward the door. The temple courtyard would have been noisy and full of people. The couple with the baby would have been in no way exceptional. But, immediately, Simeon recognized them as the answer to all his prayers.

Joseph and Mary might have expected to wait in line to be seen, the offering of two turtledoves would need to be made, but Simeon ignored the formalities. He went straight to Jesus, raised Him up, and praised God. If the angelic messages and visitations by the Magi hadn't already convinced Joseph and Mary their son was something special, Simeon's greeting would surely have sealed that deal.

Perhaps unusually in a patriarchal society, Simeon's role in the story is shared by Anna, an equally devout woman. It seems that this gift is meant for both men and women, and Simeon stretched it further (if it needed stretching) by including the Gentiles as well as the Jews. Salvation had come for the whole world!

Despite having some words of prophecy to share, Simeon didn't seem at all concerned about how the rest of the story played out. He was standing in a position of complete trust. God's promise had begun to come true and he had been allowed to see it.

What a gift! To know that the future of your country—and the world—was now being directed by God personally!

Having been allowed to play his part in welcoming Jesus to the temple—in effect, welcoming Him to the wider world outside his parents' home—Simeon was supremely content to leave now. All would be well, so he could go home any time God cared to stop by and pick him up.

Remember, God Plays a Long Game

We see *holy* people and think, "Yeah, but they're different." We convince ourselves that the kind of people they are makes holiness easier for them. But that's not the way it works. Holy people are prone to the same doubts, temptations, and weaknesses the rest of us are. They just resist them for longer.

In a way, they are God's athletes. They get knocked down from time to time, but they get back up and keep moving forward. They don't sit the game out.

They know their plays will be picked apart by the coach in the heavenly dressing room, but they hope the patience, joy, and excitement with which they played will soften His heart. And they're probably right. God loves loyalty.

Forget about short-term contracts. Decide this day which team you are on for the rest of your *career*. And go long!

The Answer to Simeon's Prayer

Perhaps Simeon went home, lived a few years in gentle retirement, and died in his sleep. Perhaps God took him away that night. We don't know. We do know that his prayer was one of thanks for the completion of a promise that had become his whole life. Whichever way it worked out, Simeon was grateful, and God took him home.

In the second part of his prayer, Simeon predicted that Jesus would cause the falling and rising of many in Israel, that He would be spoken against, and that His mother's heart would be broken in the process.

He seems to have condensed the Gospels here, and we can only wonder if Mary recalled his words as she sat at the foot of the cross.

Simeon's parting message, while no doubt difficult to hear at the time, is one we can all draw comfort from. God has this all planned out in advance. We need only be patient.

Practical Prayers

- At the end of the day, before I collapse onto the bed, dear Lord, remind me that the works of the day—employment, family, and home—are also gifts from You that I would miss very much if they weren't in my life. May I take—and continue to take—a few moments to appreciate them and the one who provided them.

- God, the waiting is often the most difficult part. You promise and we hear, but as time goes on, we also doubt. Did we really hear what we thought we heard? Keep us steadfast, keep us on course, keep in our minds and hearts the absolute joy and contentment Simeon must have felt after a lifetime of waiting.

- Lord, help us not to listen to the detractors, the people with "better" ideas, the ones who tell us we are wasting our time devoting anything to You. They don't know who it is they serve. May we love them and show them a better way through our service and devotion to Your higher cause.

2

"BUT, GOD. . .I DON'T HAVE THE TOOLS!"

Praying God Chooses Someone Else for the Work

Moses said to the Lord, "Pardon your servant, Lord. I have never been eloquent, neither in the past nor since you have spoken to your servant. I am slow of speech and tongue."
The Lord said to him, "Who gave human beings their mouths? Who makes them deaf or mute? Who gives them sight or makes them blind? Is it not I, the Lord? Now go; I will help you speak and will teach you what to say."

Exodus 4:10–12 NIV

Moses was a prince of Egypt. That should have inspired confidence in any man. But it wasn't enough. If he spoke at all in the first part of the story, it was to question. When he told the Lord he was slow of speech, we can believe it.

Perhaps his status as a foundling was known in Egypt, making him feel like an outsider. He was certainly alone when he killed the Egyptian guard. Couldn't he have stopped him with a royal order? Perhaps the lack of communication skills created the frustration that boiled over on that occasion.

So he was hesitant of speech, but not slow to act. He drove away the shepherds who were bullying Zipporah and her sisters, but we are not told if he uttered a word.

Then, when he thought he might have found a place to call home after fleeing Pharaoh's court, he saw and heard things that would tie the tongue of the most eloquent orator. A bush burned without consuming itself, his staff turned into a snake, his hand became leprous and was healed, and God wanted him to lead an insurrection!

In saying, "Pardon your servant," Moses was almost saying, "Count me out. . .please."

And why wouldn't he? Egypt was the most powerful country around, and it was ruled by a man who wanted Moses dead. Why does God always seem to pick the least likely candidate for these missions?

So he pleads a stutter, a lisp, a hesitancy of some sort. As excuses go, it wasn't a bad one. The man for that task would need to be very persuasive. Some Hebrews might be willing to follow him, but many were content to stay. The many different elders would all have to be persuaded to see things Moses' way. Not only that, he would have to convince them that his way was also God's way!

God's response was sharp and to the point. It was like He was saying, "Don't tell me about your so-called infirmities. I made the mouth that is speaking these excuses. I know what it can and can't do. I just need you to man up and say 'Okay.'"

The insecurities of the fugitive foundling prince must have run deep because he asked God to send someone else, which was like saying, "Lord, you chose the wrong guy!"

God got peeved. But He also understood. He could have made Moses do this. But perhaps Moses had experienced enough traumas for a while, so God sent him a helper he would recognize—his brother, Aaron.

God, the Almighty, bent His will once again to accommodate human frailty.

It's Not about How Others See Us

Some folk don't care what other people think—usually because they are busy thinking about themselves. But for the rest of us, other people's opinions can be a real issue. Sometimes we can learn from them, but all too often we limit ourselves because of them. We worry people will judge the clothes we wear, the car we drive, the way we look, the way we speak. And that limits us in lots of subtle (and not so subtle) ways.

The question we need to ask is this—how much do I believe I am a child of God? If we really believe that, then we have to acknowledge that we are, in reality, pretty wonderful.

The justified—but graceful—confidence that comes with that fact will put other people's opinions of us firmly in their place.

The Answer to Moses' Prayer

Moses didn't believe he had a voice others would listen to. He didn't understand that God's words would do the work, even if they had to come through Moses *and* Aaron before being heard.

Aaron served his brother and his God faithfully through most of this period. They spoke to God together, and they spoke to Pharaoh together. No doubt Moses was greatly heartened by his brother's company, and eventually we only hear of Moses speaking to his people—unaided!

His people made it to the Promised Land, and the words spoken by this hesitant speaker have been heard in prayer meetings and from pulpits ever since!

Practical Prayers

- Father God, I try Your patience and I know it. I listen to the liar who tells me I am less than others, who focuses my attention on the things I am not—as if I ought to be those things! Remind me that I am enough for Your plan for my life. And those others. . .You have different plans for them.

- Dear God, I know You don't make mistakes. I look around Your creation and I see everything works, even if I don't understand how! I need to bring some of those mysteries to mind next time I think You cut a few corners in making me so I will understand that what I think of as imperfections are simply tools for Your work that I don't yet fully understand.

- Oh, Lord! I know that what is between You and me is between You and me. I can't pass it off to someone else. Whatever You ask of me, no matter how improbable or seemingly impossible, is always part of Your plan for me. In advance may I say, "Yes, Lord," and ask You to provide the courage when the time comes.

3
"LORD, I NEED YOU!"

Praying for Help in a Broken World

"But the tax collector, standing far off, would not even lift up his eyes to heaven, but beat his breast, saying, 'God, be merciful to me, a sinner!' I tell you, this man went down to his house justified, rather than the other. For everyone who exalts himself will be humbled, but the one who humbles himself will be exalted."

LUKE 18:13–14 ESV

This is a tough world to be pure and innocent in!

There's an epic battle going on around us. A broken world is being healed—kicking and screaming all the way. In the midst of this titanic struggle, what are ordinary people supposed to do?

The trouble is that it doesn't *seem* like an epic battle. It gets played out in countless, apparently unimportant, decisions—decisions the world seems to prefer we make the wrong way. Somehow, the world makes it convenient for us to choose the easy way, the way that keeps most people happy, the way that doesn't (seem to) hurt anyone. And we fall for it time and again, without really understanding whose work we are doing.

Human nature is weak and easily taken advantage of. So, why did God make it like that? Well, if it were easy, there would be no point to the victory. We wouldn't have achieved all that much.

Let's face it, though, no one likes to berate themselves as a sinner. Usually our pride will step back from that and, in annoyance at the very idea, find more excuses for our sin.

13

But when the man in Jesus' parable says, "God, be merciful to me, a sinner," it isn't so much a plea to be spared from justified wrath but a heartfelt request for help from the only source possible—our loving Father.

Sure, *sinner* is an ugly word with lots of unpleasant connotations. But we didn't eat that apple; we are just living with the consequences. Sin is the state we were born into. We were bound to fail. . .until Jesus came along and gave us another option!

You know they say that people with addiction problems have to *want* to be helped before they can *be* helped. It's the same with each of us. God isn't going to help us be greater than our nature until we accept what that nature is. But then. . . Wow!

So you fail. So you didn't tell the exact truth. So you should have done something to help that person and you didn't. So you're embarrassed by yourself, or sometimes your anger, your fear, your conceit, your. . .whatever. . .gets the best of you. So what!

Your best is yet to come. Your best will be amazing. But until then, you need a boost in all those little battles—the little battles that make up life and play a surprisingly large part in the healing of the world.

Well, you know what? All you have to do is ask. Acknowledge what God already knows: that doing life in the best way is too much for you on your own. His mercy isn't in not being angry with us; His mercy is in waiting this long to be asked and still being willing to hold out that loving, helping hand.

His Mercy Means Less Drama

The parables Jesus used weren't just plucked out of the air. Neither were they specifically about the people living in those places at that time. They are universal, and they are also specific. They are about you.

The image of the man beating his breast and pleading for mercy is dramatic, and sometimes it happens like that, but this prayer can be prayed throughout an ordinary day as well. Whenever temptation comes a-calling, whether it be in the car, at work, or with the family, you can quietly say, "It's tempting, Lord, and I am weak. Show me Your way." The more you ask the more familiar you will become with His way. You might not always follow His advice at first, but as you get more used to asking, you will also get more used to experiencing the positive result.

One especially good result being that we will, for as long as possible, avoid the need for any real breast beating.

The Answer to the Tax Collector's Prayer

Jesus tells us that the tax collector went home justified before God. He probably also felt very relieved. In a spiritual sense, it is right to submit yourself to God, but from a strictly human point of view it is also a wonderful release to be able to take your worries, your mistakes, the pressures of your life, and lay them at someone else's feet, knowing they will be well taken care of.

The tax collector was generally seen as a servant of the Romans and a betrayer of his own people. If Jesus wanted to show that God's forgiveness was for everyone, He couldn't have chosen a more difficult example. And yet God forgave him and justified him.

Practical Prayers

- Oh, dear Lord, where do I begin? But perhaps I can just begin somewhere, knowing that You already know everything and what is important is that I do begin.

- Father. . .I did wrong. It seemed right at the time. Oh, who am I kidding? It seemed convenient at the time. I am constantly falling for those too-good-to-be-true promises. Help me remember them and recognize them for what they are. Raise me up, Lord, to be better than that.

- God. Are You still there? After all I have done? Are You sure You saw all that stuff? And You're still there. How can I possibly be worth all that to You? But it seems like I am. So, maybe we should talk together more often. You up for that? Thank You. Thank You. Thank You.

4

"JESUS, I AM UNDESERVING. BUT. . .CAN WE TALK?"

Praying from Rock Bottom

And he said unto Jesus, Lord, remember me when thou comest into thy kingdom. And Jesus said unto him, Verily I say unto thee, Today shalt thou be with me in paradise.

LUKE 23:42–43 KJV

Wouldn't prayer be easier if you could see who you were praying to and hear the reply with your own ears?

Moses did it, and he had to veil his face afterward. Saul did it (sort of), and he was blinded and terrified. The thief on the cross did it, but he had to be crucified first.

The words of the crucified thief might not always be regarded as a prayer, but let's look again. He acknowledged the innocence of the man next to him, invoked the fear of God, and fully accepted that Jesus was going to His kingdom. He had one request—that he be remembered in that kingdom.

What a humble request that was. Not to be saved, but simply to be remembered.

He believed, there and then, that this beaten and dying man was God and was the possessor of a mighty power and called Him "Lord." Which is, of course, why Jesus took on human form—so we would understand the intimacy of our relationship with God. So we could identify with Him in our time of trouble.

Seeing someone he could speak to, someone he might ask mercy of when the world had none to offer him, he asked to be remembered. Perhaps being remembered by God was all the immortality he could possibly hope for.

Three Gospels identify this man and his companion as robbers and criminals. In some translations, they are referred to as bandits. Most likely they made their living attacking and robbing travelers. The Romans, with their focus on commerce and taxation, would permit none of that when they could help it. The Jewish people would have had no sympathy for men who robbed their own. These are the most unsympathetic, undeserving characters you could find.

And they depict us at our worst—as sinners. At the end, one mocks Christ and dies. But the other one turns to Him and is accepted, despite having nothing to offer and being completely undeserving. This is the choice each of us faces and the perfect example of God's grace.

The words of the thief—his prayer—show us how approachable Jesus is. Exalted and powerful but not "high and mighty" in the pejorative sense, He is there for us in our darkest hour, no matter how low our lives have sunk. We need only to turn to Him. We might not see Him bleeding for us as the thief on the cross did, but our conversation will be no less intimate and no less effective.

The Impossible Deal

This man got paradise! What did he give as his part of that incredible deal? What did God ask of him?

He would have been almost naked—all his possessions would already have been confiscated. His worldly possessions, right then, were pain, iron spikes through his hands and feet, and a few hours of increasingly labored breathing. He swapped that—plus one important thing—for paradise. And God was pleased with the deal.

That one important thing was his acceptance that Jesus Christ was his Lord and Savior. How much weight do you think his earthly sins carried against a pedigree like that? They were washed away instantly and he was home!

Given that at the end we won't have anything more to offer, we have to ask, what does Jesus get—or want—out of such a ridiculously uneven deal?

He gets you. And that's all He ever wanted.

The Answer to the Thief's Prayer

So. . .Jesus died, and the thief died. Not necessarily in that order.

Before Jesus died, He assured the thief he would be in paradise that day. Verily! Or, absolutely!

But He died. So, how could He take anyone to paradise?

Opinions differ on what happened next. But three days later, something happened that gave twelve ordinary men the courage to live and die for the same cause. It was witnessed shortly afterward, the apostle Paul tells us, by more than five hundred people. And it started a religion that swept the globe. Jesus came back!

The thief. . .well, we hear no more about him. But for three days Jesus was not in this world. Neither is paradise.

And the thief would have been their one-man welcoming committee.

Talk about being redeemed! Talk about being raised up! Talk about an answer to prayer!

Practical Prayers

- Dear Lord, we hear the words. We are told time and again that You redeem sinners. Some folk have a hard time accepting themselves as sinners. Me? I have a hard time accepting that You will accept a sinner like me. But You do, and You do, and You do, and my tears are my thanks.

- Lord Jesus, I will come to You. When I get myself sorted out. When I get a grip on my temper. . .when I give up drinking. . .when I am too old for lustful thoughts. . .once I kick the habit. I have used all of those delaying tactics. But if the thief on the cross teaches me anything, it is that they are just excuses. I can come to You as I am. And You will still love me.

- The thief turned his head from his partner in crime to his salvation. A simple thing, but not easy. Lord, give me the strength to turn my mind from my sins to my Redeemer.

5

"I TRUST YOU, LORD—
BUT I'M IN TROUBLE!"

A Prayer of Doubt and Fear

"Lord," Ananias answered, "I have heard many reports about this man and all the harm he has done to your holy people in Jerusalem. And he has come here with authority from the chief priests to arrest all who call on your name."

ACTS 9:13–14 NIV

What happened to Saul on the road to Damascus was undoubtedly a major news story. But it almost completely overshadowed another wonderful example of faith.

After Jesus appeared to him, Saul found his world turned upside down and his sight taken away. He would go on to do an epic work for the faith, but at that point he was still regarded as a mortal enemy of the Christians. In reality, at that point he was no use, or threat, to anyone. For him to begin his new life properly, someone had to bring him back into the light.

God apparently told Paul that Ananias would come to him before He mentioned the idea to Ananias.

Now Ananias was known as a good man. Paul had been a determined persecutor and may have been complicit in murder. Rumors of his wrath would certainly have preceded him. You can understand Ananias not being in a hurry to meet him.

So once Ananias heard what the Lord had in mind, he asked something like, "Lord, You are kidding, right?" It was an all-too-human hesitation, but God wasn't playing. "Go!" He replied. And

Ananias, to his great credit, went. No more questions. He walked off to help a man he believed might possibly have him arrested or killed.

His hesitancy and his compliance had already been seen by God before He even spoke to Ananias. God probably already knew how that particular conversation would pan out even before Saul landed in the dirt. Isn't that a reassuring thought?

What must have gone through Ananias's mind on that journey? How tempted must he have been to argue with the Lord or simply to turn back? But he kept on going, as God knew he would. And when he arrived at the house on Straight Street (because this was no vague feeling he had, God had given him an actual address), he greeted Saul/Paul, laid a hand on him, and called him brother. There was courage! There was faith!

It is completely understandable that Paul's conversion story gets all the attention. After all, through him a faith that might have stayed in Jerusalem became known to the world.

But Ananias, a man of good faith and not a little courage, helped make that possible.

When You Said Love Your Enemy, Lord. . .

There are few better examples of Jesus' command to love our enemy than this one.

Saul of Tarsus was from a wealthy family, he had a high-powered education, and as a Roman and a Pharisee he was very much a part of "the establishment." He had sought special permission to harass the Christians, and he stood by holding the robes of those who stoned at least one Christian (Stephen) to death.

Now Ananias was a good man and respected among the Jews, but to Saul he would have been an insurrectionist, an evil to be rooted out.

Turn that scenario about any way you like. Imagine any kind of fear-based enmity. None of them will be more likely to have a happy ending than this one. There was no earthly possibility these two men were going to get along. But then love reached out.

It was unlikely. For Ananias, it was a scary path to walk. But he took God's love with him, and the impossible became possible.

The same outcome is possible in any kind of conflict situation. What is needed—what is always needed—is love, and someone to deliver it.

The Answer to Ananias' Prayer

Let's lay aside the great work Paul would go on to perform. That wasn't what Ananias prayed about. Ananias just wanted God to confirm what He seemed to be saying. And, although it isn't mentioned, he may have been hoping for courage to carry out the crazy-sounding task God had given him.

So what happened when he walked into that room and met a man who was his enemy—a man who had been blasted off his horse, been blinded, and had spent the last three days praying and not eating?

What would you expect in that situation? Probably nothing rational or safe.

But Ananias reached out to the persecutor, laid a hand on him, called him brother (probably with his heart in his boots), and the man's sight was restored. Paul started eating again. The two men traveled—in what we can only assume was friendly company—to visit the other disciples.

Ananias's enemy was his enemy no more.

Practical Prayers

- Oh, Lord. You have been there for me so many times. But still when You ask me to step outside my comfort zone, I hesitate, I fear. I appreciate Your patience, Lord, and Your understanding.

- Help me, Father, to understand that my enemy is not Your enemy. In fact, my enemy may not be an enemy at all, just one of Your works in progress. If I approach them in fear, I risk driving them away and undermining Your work. If I approach them in love, well. . .Thy will *will* be done.

- Lord, You are a God of second chances, as You proved when You sent Your Son to save this sorry world. May I remember the importance You place on redemption and being reborn and on healing when I encounter someone I instinctively regard as a lost cause. Going on my abilities, they may well be—and remain—a lost cause. Teach me to approach such situations and such people relying always on Your abilities.

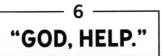

6

"GOD, HELP."

A Prayer for Wisdom

"Now, LORD my God, you have made your servant king in place of my father David. But I am only a little child and do not know how to carry out my duties. Your servant is here among the people you have chosen, a great people, too numerous to count or number. So give your servant a discerning heart to govern your people and to distinguish between right and wrong. For who is able to govern this great people of yours?"

1 KINGS 3:7–9 NIV

Solomon was the king of Israel. He was a good choice, and although the country had been through a civil war of sorts, there had been peace and prosperity for a long time.

But some wounds take a long time to heal, and Solomon found himself tidying up the loose ends of King David's reign in the bloodiest fashion. He broke a promise to his mother, had his brother killed, sent someone to slaughter his father's general by the altar, exiled Abiathar the priest, and finally killed Shimei, an enemy his father told him to kill years before.

After this bloody spree, he entered into an alliance with Egypt. But having such a powerful partner doesn't seem to have assured Solomon much.

He may have been waiting to see whether the next attack would come from home or abroad, and in an attempt to keep everyone happy, he was still sacrificing to pagan deities—despite his father's relationship with God!

God, though, seems not to have taken it personally. He still offered Solomon his heart's desire.

A hundred earthly gifts must have come to mind: greater armed might, protection from enemies, increased gold in his treasury, secure borders, fortified cities. But instead of building up his strengths through this heavenly offer, Solomon focused on his weakness.

He asked for help. And he was already smart enough to know that his best bet lay in going God's way.

"Okay, Lord," he said, "I have these people of Yours to rule over and guide. I'm asking You to give me the smarts to lead them in the way that You want them led."

Rather than worldly things, Solomon asked for wisdom, which many saw as an attribute of God. In effect he said, "Here are my life and my kingdom. Here is every decision and dilemma I will have to face concerning them. Give me Your answer to them all."

Recognizing that he didn't have all the answers was probably the smartest thing Solomon ever did.

Forever a First Timer

So we don't have a kingdom to offer to God. (Or if you do, then please accept my apologies, Your Majesty.) But we do have these lives, we do have these bodies. If we want to be wise in how we "rule" them, we should ask God how He wants us to rule them.

How many of us came from a generation where it seemed our parents must have had a Book of Rules when it came to being a Mom or Dad? But, of course, they were figuring it out for themselves too, with no instruction manual in sight. No matter what age we might be, this is our first attempt at being a human. There was no practice run, there will be no do-over.

Solomon, although raised as a prince, had never had to face the realities and responsibilities of kingship before, so he turned to God and said, "I am only a little child and do not know how to carry out my duties." His rank didn't come with an instruction manual.

So, he turned—as we can for every decision about our lives—to the one unfailing source of wisdom. Not Wikipedia. God. And the "instruction manual" that is His Book.

The Answer to Solomon's Prayer

God offered Solomon "whatever you want me to give you." There were no conditions.

If Solomon had asked for worldly things, God would have given them. He may have added a word of advice or regret, but He would have given them.

But because Solomon asked for wisdom to better carry out the divine will, God was delighted. The Lord gave Solomon what he asked for—and more. He added riches and honor and promised there would be no king like Solomon.

The only condition came in the words "if you walk in obedience to me and keep my decrees and commands as David your father did, I will give you a long life." But this was an added bonus. Solomon got his request regardless.

And he has been remembered as a king without equal. His fame spread in his own lifetime. The fabulous Queen of Sheba would later visit to see if Solomon was as wise and wonderful as she had heard. And Solomon is probably even more famous now. God kept His part of the bargain.

Solomon, on the other hand, made some poor decisions of his own—he failed to rely on the Lord's guidance, and Israel was divided after his death because of it.

Practical Prayers

- Lord, who am I to think I know what I am doing? This is my first time here. May I always remember I am here to learn about love, that is, to learn about You. Keep my ears open and my attention turned toward You. Because it's when I think I know best that I fall.

- What have You not seen, Lord? What has happened in some corner of the world, in some relationship, throughout the countless generations, that You have not seen? Father God, You have seen every possible situation I might face and every decision I might conceivably have to make played out more times than I can comprehend. My greatest wisdom will always be in turning to You for advice.

- Dear Lord, I didn't make this body. I didn't fire the spark of life within it. Any intelligence I might claim to have was always there for me to work with—but I didn't create it. So what makes me think I should have the final say on where it goes and what it does? Take my life, Lord—every detail.

7

"JESUS, WE WANT TO SEE YOU!"

A Prayer for Mercy

And when Jesus departed thence, two blind men followed him, crying, and saying, Thou son of David, have mercy on us. And when he was come into the house, the blind men came to him: and Jesus saith unto them, Believe ye that I am able to do this? They said unto him, Yea, Lord. Then touched he their eyes, saying, According to your faith be it unto you.

MATTHEW 9:27–29 KJV

Jesus was on a roll! He had calmed a storm, healed a paralytic, raised a girl from the dead, cured a woman of her incessant bleeding, and He was about to drive out a demon.

In the midst of all this, two blind men started following Him and calling after Him. Imagine what that must have been like. Perhaps they were following the noise of the crowd, but the excited crowd itself would have been an extra hazard in their way. They pushed on without being able to see the ground beneath their feet.

And Jesus, for whatever reason, didn't make it easy for them. He didn't turn and go to them. He went into a house and, somehow, they found Him there.

We aren't told if someone guided them, but somehow they found their way through the melee to this personal audience. Someone wanted them to be exactly where they were.

Then He showed that He had heard them when they shouted by asking if they believed He could do this thing. Not everyone He healed had to express belief before they were healed. The man possessed by a demon could not speak, so he could not declare his belief. The girl He had raised from the dead may never have heard of Him, let alone proclaimed her belief. That didn't stop Jesus in His mercy.

But, for some reason, He asked these two men. There and then, in that quiet place and before that all-knowing judge, they had to declare their position.

Then He reached out to them, telling them that what they were about to receive was strictly in relation to their faith. What must have gone through their minds in that instant?

We Have Eyes to See—But Do We Want to Look?

It's different now, thankfully, but being blind in that time and place would have condemned these men to a life of dependence. Perhaps they were cared for by family, perhaps they were beggars. Being healed didn't just restore their sight—it transformed their lives in a way that some might not appreciate.

Now they could see the faces of loved ones, spot difficulties before they arrived, fully enjoy the beauties of this world. . .but they would also be expected to work for a living, pay taxes, help support others, do their bit for the community, and so on.

In the more tiring days to come, they might look back to the days of dependence on others with nostalgia.

Have you ever wondered why some people seem so antagonistic to the truth? It makes no sense to be so negative about such good news. Unless part of them knows their lives will never be the same again—and they are scared. So they stay dependent on the world.

It can be a scary walk for those of us who have seen the light as well—but the joy should be worth the struggle. How that balance works out, whether the fear dilutes the joy or the joy transforms everything else—how you see God's creation—will be His gift to you "according to your faith."

The Answer to the Blind Men's Prayer

They were healed! That is the obvious answer.

Their sight was restored. They then went running around the countryside telling everyone about Jesus (despite Him telling them not to). In effect, they became missionaries. How that would have impacted their lives is anyone's guess.

Perhaps it's not surprising that they were so enthusiastic over restored sight. What's more surprising is that those who have that astounding miracle every day of their lives take it so much for granted.

But there might have been a deeper answer to their prayer. According to Matthew, the blind men didn't actually ask for their sight to be restored. They asked for mercy. When Jesus asked if they believed He could do this, He didn't specify what "this" was. Perhaps their sight was an added bonus. Perhaps the real answer to their prayer—and what each of us must hope for above all else—was His mercy.

Practical Prayers

- Dear Lord, "through a glass darkly" is a fair assessment of how I see Your plan for me. But it isn't You who darkens the glass. It's my own fears, my own desires. . .it's me. Stay with me as I try to clear the lenses of my perception that I might see Your will ever more clearly.

- Lord Jesus, we humans complicate things! I'm sorry on behalf of us all. But You are the great simplifier—if only we would listen. Do I believe? Yes—but. Those buts, those doubts, are the work of the world, the work of the enemy, the work of my fallen nature. And I know You don't want any of those complications. You simply want me to simply believe.

- Oh, my Savior. Those blind men heard You and found You in the midst of what must have seemed like a victory parade. People surrounded You, having all sorts of expectations or just wanting to be part of the crowd. But the blind men asked You for nothing more than mercy. May I have sight enough to see that, in the midst of the noise and chaos of this life, Your mercy is all I need.

8

"ALMIGHTY GOD, I'M UNDER ATTACK. STRENGTHEN MY NERVES AND STEADY MY HANDS."

A Prayer for Steadfastness

Then I sent unto him, saying, There are no such things done as thou sayest, but thou feignest them out of thine own heart. For they all made us afraid, saying, Their hands shall be weakened from the work, that it be not done. Now therefore, O God, strengthen my hands.

NEHEMIAH 6:8–9 KJV

While in the comfort of the court of King Artaxerxes, Nehemiah had it in mind to do a great work for God—but things didn't go smoothly once he was out there in the real world.

God had scattered the people of Israel, and many of them were pressed into the service of foreign rulers. But the time had come for Him to bring His humbled people back to the Promised Land.

The first thing they needed was a rallying point. The temple in Jerusalem would be that rallying point. But Jerusalem itself was in ruins and undefended.

Nehemiah, a Jew in service to the king of Persia, asked royal permission to go to Jerusalem and rebuild those walls. Pushing his luck more than just a little, he also asked the king to provide men and materials for the work. God must have softened Artaxerxes' heart because, amazingly, he gave a humble cupbearer all of these things.

Once at Jerusalem, Nehemiah had to convince the local populace this was a task worth undertaking. But not everyone was happy with the idea. His opponents didn't just come from inside the ruined walls—the local rulers weren't happy about it, either. They feared a defended Jerusalem might be a focus for rebellion against them and weaken their power in the area.

So, the psychological warfare began.

Nehemiah was never short of people telling him he was bringing doom upon them. Eventually half his workforce was standing guard against the expected attacks while the other half built walls and hung gates.

The attack didn't come, but the fear-induced squabbles would have been debilitating to everyone involved. The safer option of walking away must have been in many people's minds.

And remember, these people were not builders. They were Jews who had returned from the great exile. They had families to provide for while they built this wall (which had to be built quickly before it was attacked). They would often have been physically and mentally exhausted.

Nehemiah must have felt so very alone at times, and he knew more than anyone how vulnerable they really were. So he turned to God and prayed that tired hands would be given new strength.

It Seemed Like a Good Idea at the Time

There are lots of things we know we *should* do.

It was every devout Jew's duty to return to the Holy Land if they could, even if just to worship at the newly rebuilt temple but. . .you know. . .life gets in the way.

Nehemiah resolved to do a mighty work—while he was in the palace. But many hundreds of miles away from his royal protection and surrounded by rulers who only had to leave no survivors to get away with their actions, that mighty work must have often seemed like a much less attractive prospect.

Now relate that to your life. How many times have you set out with the best of intentions to be the person God wants you to be? You know it's a righteous thing. You know you will be better for it. But once you start, the doubts and distractions set to work. You are assailed from within and from without. And you gradually forget the good feeling you started off with. The point of it all gets buried under the complications.

Nehemiah understood that feeling.

So do that mighty work in your life, and when you get to the giving-up point, do what Nehemiah did. Finish the work!

The Answer to Nehemiah's Prayer

Amazingly—or perhaps not so amazingly if you believe in the power of prayer—the walls were built in record time, the temple was protected, and the Jewish people had a home to come back to. The time of exile, long prayed for, was nearing its end.

The people managed to put aside their squabbles and work together. The feared attacks didn't happen. God strengthened Nehemiah's hands in more ways than one.

More than that, it was seen that a powerful earthly force and a powerful heavenly force backed this construction project.

Of course, the point of it all was that God was bringing His people home, and He wasn't going to leave that home undefended. Nehemiah was His instrument in bringing that about. And Nehemiah's faith was what made him such an effective part of the Lord's plan.

Practical Prayers

- Time and again, Lord, I know what I ought to do—and fail to do it. Remind me when I need it that Nehemiah was no bricklayer; he was no construction engineer. He had probably never done a day's manual labor in his life. But he knew there was work waiting there for him to do, and he set out in faith and trust. Now if he could do that with Your help. . .

- Lord, I might as well call the fears I suffer from "Shemaiah." He was sent by Nehemiah's enemies to discourage him and discredit him. My fears—when they contradict Your will for my life—are no doubt sent by Your enemy for the same purpose. Shemaiah, I am calling your bluff!

- Lord, with Your help ordinary people built a fortified wall around a city in fifty-two days. No wonder Nehemiah's enemies were astounded and afraid. I know I also have the capacity to astound—if I live my life the way You would have me live it. May I lay a brick in the building of a godly future today, and another tomorrow, and another the next day. . .

9

"IF YOU DON'T DO THIS WITH ME, LORD, THEN IT'S NOT WORTH DOING."

A Prayer for the Presence of God

Moses said to the LORD, "See, you say to me, 'Bring up this people,' but you have not let me know whom you will send with me. Yet you have said, 'I know you by name, and you have also found favor in my sight.' Now therefore, if I have found favor in your sight, please show me now your ways, that I may know you in order to find favor in your sight. Consider too that this nation is your people."

EXODUS 33:12–13 ESV

"God be with you," we sometimes say. But imagine if God Himself replied, "No! No, I won't be!"

Devastating or what?

Well, that's pretty much what God said to the Israelites.

He had taken them from slavery in Egypt. He had promised them homes in the land of milk and honey. An angel was sent ahead of them to clear the way. But God couldn't bear to go with them Himself.

Despite the plagues He sent on Egypt, despite the parting of the Red Sea, the Israelites still insisted on worshipping false idols. God was so hurt by their behavior He feared He might lash out and destroy them if He stayed too close. So, He planned to take Himself away from them—for their own safety and, no doubt, for His peace of mind.

Moses, who had been thrust into an unwanted leadership role, was wise enough to know that he wasn't the real leader. If this mass migration depended on him, it would fail. If the chosen people of God didn't have God with them, then they would fail.

"How am I going to learn how You want this done," he asked, "if You aren't there telling me?"

So, while the Israelites were beating themselves up over the news, Moses did the smart thing and kept the lines of communication open. He pitched the Tent of Meeting outside the camp, a place where God didn't have to be with the Israelites—but where He wasn't too far removed, either.

They kept talking, and Moses reminded God (if He needed reminding and if this wasn't part of His plan all along) that He did, after all, love the Israelites and that the plans He had for them would fall flat if He wasn't there to hold them up. Plus, if they failed, if they died in the desert, if they couldn't beat the Canaanites, or if Egypt claimed them back, how would that affect the way the rest of the world saw their Lord?

Meanwhile, as the peace talks continued, the rest of the Israelites had an opportunity to contemplate a life without God.

Building Your Own Tent of Meeting

Have you ever walked away in frustration?

Very few things gnaw at you like that feeling. You feel (probably rightly) that you have been pushed beyond all reasonable limits. But there's more to it. Justified or not, you have broken a relationship.

And the God you serve is all about relationships. Of course, safety is a big consideration and probably the only thing that truly justifies walking away. But let's face it, most of our walk aways are over smaller things—annoyances, frustrations—and they say as much about us as the people who inspire them.

If we take the exchange at face value, Moses reminds God that He is better than that—that the result of it all is worth a little more effort.

In some situations, leaving is the only thing to do. There's no denying that. But if there is a realistic chance of a better outcome, part of you is always going to regret not taking it.

So build your own version of the Tent of Meeting, whether in physical space or in your head. Remove yourself, but not too far. Take the time to talk to God about it.

He has, literally, been there. When He suggests a way to move on from there, you can believe it comes from His heart.

The Answer to Moses' Prayer

God granted Moses' prayer. He traveled with the Israelites in person. . .if you can call a pillar of smoke and a column of fire "in person."

Moses got to look upon his Lord and was eventually buried by Him. Their relationship wasn't an easy one, but it was a mighty work they were undertaking and they did it together.

Neither the Israelites nor their leader obeyed God absolutely, and their way was more difficult because of it. How like life is that?

The Israelites, despite this scare, continued to try the Lord's patience. Some of us never learn. He never left them but did, from time to time, turn them over to their enemies as a reminder of how much they needed Him.

Even in their captivity, though, He was with them.

Practical Prayers

- Lord, there have been times I complained You weren't there for me. Usually the complaints were a shield that hid behaviors of mine that You wouldn't be part of. But if You really weren't there. . .well. . .I don't have to contemplate that because I know You always are.

- Heavenly Father, it's easy to complain. It's easy to be the naysayer or the idol worshipper. The weight on the shoulders of those trying to do it right is often immense, be they parents, elected officials, religious leaders—or You! May I never be the one to take the easy way, adding to their burdens in the process.

- Dear God, my journey through life toward my heavenly home may never feature in a holy book like the Exodus did. I doubt anyone will ever make a movie out of it. But it's pretty important to me. And, here and now, I acknowledge I can't make the journey without You. Be my guide at every turn, Lord.

10

"LORD, YOU SAVED US—AND I NEED TO SING ABOUT IT!"

A Prayer of Thanks

*"That the leaders took the lead in Israel, that the people
offered themselves willingly, bless the LORD! Hear,
O kings; give ear, O princes; to the LORD I will sing;
I will make melody to the LORD, the God of Israel."*

JUDGES 5:2–3 ESV

The theory went like this—with the people of God following the commandments of God, there was no need for kings. It might seem like a fine theory—if you've never met any real-life people!

After Moses and Joshua went to their eternal rewards, the Israelites tended to return to their old pagan ways and, as a result, were regularly beaten up by their enemies. God raised up judges, generally wise men, who would settle disputes and remind the people of the ways of the Lord.

Deborah, as far as we know, was the only woman to hold the post in biblical times. And she lived in turbulent times. The Promised Land was once again under the rule of its enemies, and Deborah said, "Enough!" This situation, she knew, was not God's will. At least not while God's people were being faithful.

She sent for Barak of Naphtali and told him the time had come. God had told her that he, Barak, was to lead the people against their oppressor.

Well, how would you feel? Barak wasn't keen—but he went. A great victory was won but, because of Barak's hesitation, the majority of the glory went to a woman, Jael, who killed the enemy general by spiking him through the head. Both men's pride would have been hurt by that, but only Barak lived to deal with the embarrassment.

He didn't let it stop him from joining in the celebration, though. After the campaign was completed and twenty years of oppression was brought to an end, Deborah offered up a song/prayer of thanks to God for their deliverance. And Barak sang alongside her.

The Song of Deborah was a retelling of the war and how God won it. It was meant to be listened to and sung again in distant towns and villages. It praised those who helped, questioned those who hesitated, recounted how even the land and the heavens had joined in, and Barak and Jael were praised, but most of all it sang of what might be achieved when God's people followed their Lord.

It's a thought well worth considering. Even today.

Follow a Leader Who Is Being Led

I hope you never have cause to raise an army against oppressive neighbors, let alone thank God for vanquishing them. Unless you actually are in the armed forces, inviting them over for dinner and a chat might be a better way to go.

So what can we take from this ode to victory in battle?

Well, there's a secondary theme to the prayer that has nothing to do with war and is very applicable to modern life.

Deborah began her song by celebrating the fact that the leaders of Israel took responsibility and the people played their part. And she made it plain that the motivating factor was God's will.

If the people are against the leaders and the leaders are against the people, a country—any country—will tear itself apart. What you need is for everyone to fulfill their role and for their role to be a godly one. If you are following a leader, make sure he or she is following God. If you would lead, even in your own family, make sure you are leading along the path set out by the Lord.

In our own capacity, whatever that may be, we need to step up. Even if we hesitate like Barak did, we still need to answer that call.

Imagine what a difference that would make to the world!

The Answer to Deborah's Prayer

"And the land had rest for forty years."

Given that Deborah was already a married woman of some renown at the beginning of the war, the following forty years may well have coincided with the remainder of her life. The book of Judges had already said that there were times of peace and prosperity while individual judges lived, but the people rapidly reverted to paganism when they died.

Well, the same thing happened after the time of Deborah. Once again they turned to other gods, once again foreign rulers oppressed them. I mean, really? These guys raised being a "stiff-necked people" to an art form.

Eventually they cried out to God again. Then He sent a prophet. Then He sent an angel. Then He sent a farm boy called Gideon.

Practical Prayers

- Dear Lord, I take my victories for granted and often forget to thank You. But I don't ask You to forgive my forgetfulness. Because it isn't really forgetfulness, is it? It's more likely that what I call a victory will often be something I would be embarrassed to bring to You. Earthly, human, petty, even vindictive things. Lord, make my idea of a victory the same as Yours—which means, of course, something achieved in love!

- Sing? Sing? Heavenly Father, I like the idea of singing Your praises but, outside of church, I am just not that person. David did it, Deborah did it, but others had different styles. So, Lord, may I substitute a joyous life, where everyone knows the source of my joy, for singing in public? Thank you! (Joyously Yours!)

- Lord, Deborah took the lead and Barak faltered. But he did his best to catch up. And, at the end, they sang the victory song together. If I find myself calling others, may I be graceful with their failings. If I find myself called but not ready, may I remember that how I run the end of my race has still to be decided, and a late start is always better than no start.

11

"GOD, I'M NOT SURE WHO YOU ARE. BUT I'M PREPARED TO LISTEN!"

The Prayer of a Novice

Therefore Eli said to Samuel, "Go, lie down, and if he calls you, you shall say, 'Speak, Lord, for your servant hears.'" So Samuel went and lay down in his place. And the Lord came and stood, calling as at other times, "Samuel! Samuel!" And Samuel said, "Speak, for your servant hears."

1 Samuel 3:9–10 esv

Eli wasn't a bad man. He wanted to be God's man. But he was weak when it came to his sons and their abuse of power.

The boys were rapists and thieves. No one could stand against them because of their position in the temple. Eli had given them a talking to, but they ignored the old man. People suffered because of their actions and his inaction. His blindness to their continued blasphemies seemed to be mirrored by his failing eyesight. The time had come for a more effective replacement.

Samuel was a child. His mother, Hannah, had dedicated him to the temple as an offering of thanks for his life as soon as he was weaned. He was a servant to Eli, who seems to have treated him kindly. But, despite serving in the temple, he had yet to have any personal experience of the Lord. God, however, already knew He was going to do mighty works through Hannah's son.

Samuel was asleep when God called him. Waking up and recognizing the voice of authority, young Samuel ran to the only lord he knew—Eli. Eli sent him back to bed, but when it happened again and again, Eli showed his heart and his faith.

Understanding that God wanted to talk to the servant rather than the high priest, Eli put his pride aside and prepared Samuel for the encounter.

Just how do you prepare for an encounter with God? According to Eli, you stand up and say, "I am Your servant and I am listening." And that was exactly what God wanted to hear from Samuel.

The prayer ended there. God did the rest of the talking. We have to wonder if respectful listening might not also be a form of prayer.

God told Samuel how he was going to turn Eli's world upside down for the sake of Israel. Eli slept nearby and didn't stir. When God finished talking, the boy went back to sleep.

In the morning, the high priest asked his servant what the Lord had said. Then he showed his faith one more time. Instead of railing against the unfairness of the downfall God had in mind for his house, Eli offered up what might almost be called a prayer in its own right. He said, "He is the Lord; let him do what is good in his eyes" (1 Samuel 3:18 NIV).

Of course, if Eli had done what was good in God's eyes, he might have been a happier man.

While Things Are Still Quiet

God spoke to Samuel when the boy was asleep.

Given the pace of modern life, it might seem that the sleeping hours are all we have to spare for God. That might be His best chance to catch our attention.

Of course, He can get our attention at any time, and the upheaval that might involve will usually depend on how well we have been listening beforehand.

It makes sense to seek out the voice of the Lord while the matters He wants to address are still small, rather than wait until He has to put His foot down.

So actively create a space and a time in your life where you can shut out the noise of the world, lay aside the cares of the day, open your heart and say, "Your servant is listening, Lord."

The Answer to Samuel's Prayer

Eli's sons were killed in battle, and when he heard the news, Eli, blind and in his nineties, fell and broke his neck. Their line had come to an end.

Samuel's reputation as a prophet grew, and his willingness to listen meant God talked to him often. He appointed Saul as king, anointed David as Saul's successor, and when he died, even though there was a civil war going on, it is told that the entire country gathered to mourn him.

Strangely for such a wise man, he seems to have followed old Eli's example in one thing. He appointed his sons as judges to succeed him. They, like Eli's boys, abused their position. So much so that the people of Israel declared they had had enough of judges and wanted a king.

Both Samuel and God agreed that this was a bad move. But Saul was crowned, almost as a lesson to the people to be careful what they wished for.

Despite the situation with his sons, Samuel ended his life highly regarded as a man who listened to his Lord.

Practical Prayers

- Dear Lord, there are many earthly masters claiming my allegiance. They call on me in many ways with many voices. And this life is such that I often have to answer them. But if what they demand of me is other than Your will, then may I hear another voice—Your voice—and may I recognize it so I might stand up and say, "Shhh. The Lord is talking now. And I am listening."

- Father God, You answer our prayers, often by putting the right people in the right place at the right time. They also obey Your will, whether they know it or not. Eli didn't hear Your voice, but he knew he had a part to play in this work of Yours. May I understand that You have other prayers in need of answering as well, and when I hear You speak to another, may I put myself where You need me to be, for their sake and Yours.

- I am listening—even though I find it difficult to believe You are talking to me. I am listening—even though I can't imagine what You are saying is possible. I am listening—even though I find what You say difficult to understand. In whatever situation, dear Lord, may I always be able to say that one thing. I am listening.

12

"LORD, GIVE ME A CHILD—AND I WILL GIVE HIM BACK TO YOU!"

A Prayer for Fulfillment

And she vowed a vow and said, "O Lord of hosts, if you will indeed look on the affliction of your servant and remember me and not forget your servant, but will give to your servant a son, then I will give him to the Lord all the days of his life, and no razor shall touch his head."

1 Samuel 1:11 esv

Could you give away a child?

I don't mean on those days when they refuse to tidy their bedrooms and insist you have no idea what they are going through. I mean when they are still little, innocent, and only just learning to feed themselves.

Hannah did.

But why?

And how could that possibly be a good thing?

Because she remembered how Samuel was given to her.

As one of the two wives of Elkanah, and the childless one of the two, she was regularly humiliated and ridiculed by Elkanah's other wife. He did his best to reassure her she was loved. But in that place at that time, children were a visible measure of a woman's worth. She felt worthless and her "co-wife" reinforced that feeling.

Elkanah gave her his love and gave her extra food to show his favor, but his other wife's scorn made all of that seem like nothing. Perhaps the other wife piled on the pain because she knew Hannah had Elkanah's heart and she resented it.

Like a foolish man, Elkanah asked his upset wife if he wasn't better to her than ten sons. To his credit, he seems to have taken the hint. A child by her husband was the thing Hannah desired—even needed—the most.

So she prayed. She prayed that if God gave her a son, she would give him back; her child would have "no razor. . .touch his head," which meant he would be a Nazirite, one set apart and dedicated to God, a priest! She wanted her heart's desire, but she also wanted it to be God's heart's desire.

She prayed so fervently that Eli, the high priest, berated her for being drunk in the temple. She poured her heart, soul, and all her pain into this prayer. She was so focused on talking to God that she spared no part of her awareness for wondering how she must have looked.

Understanding her at last, Eli bade her go in peace and added his own personal prayer that God grant her what she asked for.

Praying for the Right Things

We are told that if we pray, it will be given to us. But it doesn't always work out like that. Sometimes we pray fervently for things that never come to pass. Why is that?

Well, it might be that God answers our prayers in His own time, or in His own way. But sometimes, He might just look down on us and say, "Really? You want that? I don't think so." From His vantage point in eternity, God knows all the ramifications of each answered prayer and sometimes the things we think we need aren't really the best things for us.

God wants the best for us. And He has a better idea of what is best for us than we do, so when we pray, let's make it less about what we want and more about what He wants. As it says in the Lord's Prayer—Thy will be done!

The Answer to Hannah's Prayer

Hannah's answer began with the peace she was given immediately afterward, and it carries on to this day.

After the prayer, Hannah "went her way, and did eat, and her countenance was no more sad" (1 Samuel 1:18 KJV).

Her son was given to her, and the time she spent weaning him must have been the happiest of her life thus far. Once little Samuel was eating solid food, he was delivered to the temple. How heartrending that must have been, but the promise was willingly kept.

The little boy, set apart for the Lord, would restore the dignity of the temple, lead his country, and advise its kings.

We don't know if Hannah went on to have other children, but she must have watched her son's progress and all the good he did for the Lord and been very glad she prayed that prayer.

And the lessons taught to Israel by Samuel (and his mother) are with us to this day in the pages of the Bible.

Practical Prayers

- Dear Lord, Hannah felt she needed a baby. You needed someone to restore Your people. Happily, the two coincided. May my prayers always coincide with Your plans. And if they don't, may I have the wisdom to adjust my prayers.

- Father God, the things I pray for are important to me, just like the things I wanted as a child seemed so important back then. Looking back, I am glad I didn't get everything I wanted when I wasn't smart enough to know what was best for me. Thank You, Lord, for the prayers You answer by not answering.

- Almighty God, there is nothing I have that did not come from You. My life, my children, my work, the coins in my purse or my pocket. All from You. May I be as generous in turning these things toward Your use as Hannah was. They are all Yours, anyway. I need only remember it.

13

"I'VE HIT THE BOTTOM—HELP ME COME BACK!"

A Prayer That Strength Will Arise from Despair

"Simon, Simon, Satan has asked to sift all of you as wheat. But I have prayed for you, Simon, that your faith may not fail. And when you have turned back, strengthen your brothers." But he replied, "Lord, I am ready to go with you to prison and to death."

Luke 22:31–33 NIV

The disciples were about to be thrown to the wolves!

Well, not really. God would send the Holy Spirit to empower them. Jesus would come back. But, at this point, they didn't know any of that. All they knew was that their leader was about to leave them, and the people who hated Him were unlikely to let them live after He was gone.

Now Jesus told them that Satan had also requested that he be allowed to dispose of them. Those twelve guys would have been perfectly justified in feeling the world was out to get them.

But Jesus Himself prayed for them! Why would He do that? Surely He must have known exactly what would happen. So, why the need for prayer?

It's a reminder that as all-powerful and all-knowing as God is, He chooses not to be all-controlling. Jesus, who could tell Simon Peter exactly how often he would deny his Lord, still had to trust in (and strengthen) Peter's faith for what would come after that.

He told Peter "When you have turned back. . ." but Peter didn't think to ask, "Lord, from where?" Then He prayed that Peter would strengthen his brothers.

It was a big task! Peter had the kind of macho "strength" that came from fear and insecurity. He acted tough because he was afraid to fail. But his strength was all about holding himself together and building himself up. Jesus was going to ask a lot more of him in the future, and if Peter didn't step up to the mark, the church would most likely be swept from the face of the earth.

Unaware of the full import of the Lord's words, Peter, as usual, resorted to bluster. He would stand by Jesus even unto death, he insisted. Ultimately he would, but not in any way he might have imagined.

I'm Capable—of Being Incapable!

"It's okay. I can do it!"

Sure you can. But maybe the other person needs to help, or maybe it would be a bonding thing, or perhaps it would be a teaching opportunity, helping make the other person as capable as you.

But then there is that perennial nagging voice—that voice we know we should ignore—that tells you the world is looking for signs of weakness to pounce on. So you insist you have it under control even when you don't, and all those other positive opportunities get shut down. Because of fear. Because of that little voice.

Now let's look at what you can't do. Can you grow an inch, can you heal a cut, can you turn the world on its axis? In the face of such expertise, we ought to be happy to say, "I can't do it all by myself, Lord. Help me." Because He does want to help you. But He also wants you to help Him. And so we get back to those bonding moments, those teaching opportunities.

There are times when we need to be strong, but we also need to remember that our times of weakness—whether imposed *on* us or allowed *by* us—are often when a far more capable power than us does His best work.

Jesus' Prayer Is Answered

The Lord's prayer was answered through a broken heart. But so often we need to get out of our own way before we can be what we ought to be for Him.

Peter "wept bitterly." When the courage he believed in so much had been put to the test, it had failed. Fear overwhelmed him, and he denied knowing Jesus three times. In those bitter tears must have come the realization that he wasn't the man he thought he was. In the real battle between good and evil, his own strength wasn't enough.

But his faith, strengthened by Jesus' prayer, saw him through this despair. And when word came of the possible resurrection of the Lord, Peter ran to the tomb, not caring who saw him. When Jesus was spotted on the shore while the disciples were fishing the Sea of Galilee, Peter jumped in and swam to him. The rest of his life was spent heading toward the man he had turned away from.

The impetuous, sometimes foolish man that Peter had been was reborn as a man of authority—one who would strengthen the faith of others. And the one on whom Jesus would eventually build His church.

Practical Prayers

- Lord, though my loved ones never leave my heart when they leave my sight, I am often distracted by the things of the world. It is a humbling thing to know that we are always in Your sight and always in Your prayers. May we only be worthy of the faith You place in us.

- Father God, we fear the desperate places, the places where we seem to have nothing. Often we sell our integrity to avoid them. Help us keep in mind that it is not Your intention that we go to such places unless we need to be rebuilt in a way that better serves You. In the places where we seem to have nothing, we always have You.

- At times we are all tested. At times we are all found lacking. That's just the way this life works. How we react is what makes the difference. Judas denied You and ran away to his own destruction. Peter denied You and forever after ran toward You. Judas took the way of pride. Peter took the way of faith. Even at our lowest point, may we choose faith over pride.

14

"GOOD CHAT, LORD. NOW STOP BEING SO MYSTERIOUS."

A Prayer to See the Glory of God

Then Moses said, "I pray You, show me Your glory!" And He said, "I Myself will make all My goodness pass before you, and will proclaim the name of the Lord before you; and I will be gracious to whom I will be gracious, and will show compassion on whom I will show compassion." But He said, "You cannot see My face, for no man can see Me and live!"

Exodus 33:18–20 NASB

Any conversation between a man or woman and God constitutes a prayer. Moses had taken the practice almost to the level of a chat between friends, even seeming to change the Lord's mind on occasion. With this request, though, he might have been pushing his luck. Still, that had paid off for him in the past.

God was furious with the Israelites for their worship of the golden calf. Moses hadn't been impressed, either. He took the first set of commandments God had given him and smashed them on the ground. He took the golden calf, ground it up, mixed it with water, and made the Israelites drink it! In the following battle between the idolaters and those who were on the Lord's side, three thousand men died.

All this Moses was prepared to do, but when he heard that God planned to abandon them, he thought that was going too far. He interceded on behalf of the patience-trying Israelites and seemed to have persuaded Him. God, who at one point wanted nothing more to do with His chosen people, was now willing to travel with them to the Promised Land.

Not bad for a guy who originally wanted to be excused from national leader duties due to his halting speech.

Then Moses moved beyond the current situation and asked something for himself. It wouldn't have been necessary for him in that time and place, but even that request proved to be part of God's plan.

He asked to see God's glory. Another man might have been dispatched with a lightning bolt at his heels for such familiarity, but God and Moses had established a relationship by this point. So the Lord gave him what he wanted but—as is His style—not strictly in the way Moses expected.

God's Glory? It's Not Hiding

A man stood in a wildflower meadow and said, "If You are real, God, show Yourself!" Nothing happened. And he left that meadow convinced God was real. Because he understood (or was given the understanding) that God was in everything he saw there.

Every flower, bee, blade of grass, and field mouse is complex beyond understanding. Gloriously made, in fact.

We don't need to look any further than His creation to find God, but to understand Him and draw closer to Him we need to concern ourselves with more than what He looks like. We need to know and explore what He is all about. The Ten Commandments would be a good place to begin that search. Jesus Christ would be a good place to end it (if, indeed, such a search could be ended this side of heaven).

The Bible has plenty of descriptions of God's glory. What we need to do is apply them to our lives, see what they make of us and the world around us, then understand that we too can be a part of His glory!

The Answer to Moses' Prayer

Despite their close relationship, Moses simply couldn't see the face of God. The human brain and body can only take so much. God granted Moses his request—but in a merciful way. He placed Moses in a cleft of rock for his protection, and perhaps also to limit his view. Then He swept past in all His majesty, allowing Moses to see only His departing figure.

What Moses thought of the encounter we are not told, but the physical effect on him was such that everyone who saw him knew something wonderful had happened. Moses actually glowed!

But God did more than that to show His glory. You see, His glory isn't simply in His awesome appearance; it is in what He is all about. As He appeared to Moses, He proclaimed His name—He announced Himself as merciful, gracious, long-suffering, abundant in goodness, and just. Then He and Moses hammered out (with Moses doing the actual hammering) the Ten Commandments, and this became the covenant between the Lord and His people.

Forever after, His people would know exactly what God was about—because Moses asked to see His glory.

Practical Prayers

- Almighty God, teach me patience. Your glory in this world is merely an introduction to the next. Seeing You in all Your glory should rightly be the reward of a life spent preparing for the eternal one that is to come. If I ask for shortcuts in that, I cheat myself. Replace my impatience, if You will, Lord, with excited anticipation.

- Father God, I take Your glory for granted on a daily basis, and I hope You don't mind. But, for my sake as much as anything, keep opening my eyes to Your wonders until I really understand that You are everywhere, nothing is ordinary, and that this life, with all its apparent hardships, is one long exploration of You and Your glory.

- Dear Lord, I believe Your words, Your commandments, Your covenant have the power to do mighty works in and through me. But it's a scary prospect at the same time, and the adversary is ever distracting me from the truth. Give me the courage and insight to at least begin the process, so that I, who was made in Your image, might eventually be remade in Your glory.

15

"CHOOSE YOUR MAN, LORD."

A Prayer for the Right Person

So they nominated two men: Joseph called Barsabbas (also known as Justus) and Matthias. Then they prayed, "Lord, you know everyone's heart. Show us which of these two you have chosen to take over this apostolic ministry, which Judas left to go where he belongs." Then they cast lots, and the lot fell to Matthias; so he was added to the eleven apostles.

ACTS 1:23–26 NIV

Jesus chose twelve disciples, but when it came time for those disciples to go out into the world spreading the Gospel, there were only eleven left.

Judas had handed the Lord over to the earthly powers and then taken his own life, unable to live with what he had done or to ask for forgiveness.

The number twelve was significant. Not only had Jesus chosen twelve, but there were traditionally twelve tribes of Israel—twelve aspects to God's people.

When it came time for the disciples to become apostles—to move from those learning the Way to those living the Way—Peter declared it was time to reestablish the twelve. And they weren't short of options. At one point, Jesus had sent out seventy-two "missionaries." It seems there were more than twelve from the beginning; Joseph and Matthias were said to have been with the group from the days of John the Baptist.

They must have been outstanding men of faith to be chosen from such a large group, and evenly matched as well. Perhaps the disciples were unable to choose between them, or perhaps they understood that God's specific representatives ought to be chosen by God.

The "winner" would be asked to take the place of a disgraced disciple and restore the dignity of the group as a whole. This was no small thing. Both must have been brave men to be willing to take all that on.

So the eleven disciples prayed. But the question has to be asked, did they listen? Because immediately after, we are told they cast lots—or tossed dice—presumably trusting God to control the way they fell.

It seems an odd way for men of faith to reach a decision. Perhaps it was their way of hurrying God along rather than waiting for Him to answer in His own time. Or perhaps they believed that God, who spins the planets around the sun, causes seeds to sprout in the dark earth, and gives each of us our every heartbeat, could certainly make a game of chance work out in His favor.

Pray and Stop

We say we trust in God, but how many of our old habits do we still rely on?

If we have a big decision to make and we flip a coin rather than find an answer through prayer, are we trusting God—or chance? If we really need to be somewhere and pray God helps us get there on time but then break a few traffic laws to help us along the way, who are we depending on? If we pray a situation will turn out one way and then panic when it seems to be going another way, how much confidence do we display in God's preferred outcome?

Seeking guidance by prayer isn't always easy, and the answers don't always come quickly. Sometimes God's answer appears immediately, but when it doesn't, we need to resist the temptation to hurry it along. Because that temptation is. . .well. . .a temptation. And we all know whose favorite tool that is.

Pray—and get your answer. Or pray—and wait for an answer. But once you have prayed, stop. You have given the matter over to God. If He needs your help, He will ask for it. But, mostly, He's got it covered.

The Answer to the Disciples' Prayer

God—or the fall of the dice—declared Matthias would fill the twelfth place in the band of apostles.

As with many of the band, we know little of their later lives outside popular tradition. The Bible refers to a Justus (Joseph was known as Justus) who is involved in Paul's work after this election, so perhaps he stayed active in the faith. It would be difficult to imagine a man who had such strong faith that he was considered for such a position not dedicating his life to the Lord in whatever capacity.

Tradition has Matthias preaching the gospel in Africa, where he was martyred for the cause. He probably knew this was no safe and comfortable office he was being elected to, which speaks volumes about his faith and courage.

Some commentators, though, wonder if the disciples resorted to casting lots because God didn't supply a clear-cut answer for them. Perhaps because His chosen man, Saul of Tarsus, was about to set out for Damascus, on his way to becoming the apostle to the Gentiles.

How often does it happen that God answers our prayers in His own particular way?

Practical Prayers

- Dear Lord, it mattered to You who took that twelfth space. And it matters no less to You who fills the various posts in my life. When I consider whom to trust, whom to love, whom to work for, whom to employ, may I turn first to You for guidance so my life is filled with the people You want to be there, either for my help and guidance or to challenge me and help me grow in my faith.

- Almighty God, keep my mind and heart ever open to the possibility that Your response to my prayer might be nothing like I imagined. It would be silly in the extreme to be frustrated by that, so may I choose instead to be astounded and awestruck when You exceed my expectations.

- Loving Father, the ways of the world are not Your ways—but they are what I am used to and what I resort to at times almost without thinking. They are easier—easier to do, easier to recognize, easier to blame when they don't work out. But I would walk the more difficult path: the path of patience, trust, and relying on You, the path of everlasting results rather than quick fixes. Hold my hand, Lord, and always be my guide.

16

"LORD. . .I'M A BOY! AND THEY ARE KINGS!"

A Prayer to Be Excused

Then I said, "Ah, Lord GOD! Behold, I do not know how to speak, for I am only a youth." But the LORD said to me, "Do not say, 'I am only a youth'; for to all to whom I send you, you shall go, and whatever I command you, you shall speak. Do not be afraid of them, for I am with you to deliver you, declares the LORD."

JEREMIAH 1:6–8 ESV

Jeremiah gets a bit of a bad name, being generally seen as a bearer of bad news. The fact that his life was a time of bad news wasn't his fault. He was simply the one who pointed out what the people of God were doing, what they ought to be doing, and what was going to happen if they didn't change their ways.

Being a prophet wasn't easy work for Jeremiah. The news he was sharing often had him in tears. Bad news wasn't his first choice. But God needed someone to remind His people that, spiritually, they were driving toward a cliff and a big fall was coming.

Israel and Judah were separate kingdoms at the time, but each seemed as faithless as the other. The Almighty, who had already "divorced" Israel, saw Judah following in her sister nation's footsteps. Despite being appalled by their behavior, He was still reaching out to both nations and sent a man of Judah to Israel to proclaim the message of the Lord. That message was one of anger and disappointment, but also of love and forgiveness if only the people of God would turn back to Him.

Jeremiah served God and advised three kings over the course of forty years, so when God first spoke to him in this way, he would have been very young. His "defense" that he was "only a youth" was perfectly justified. It just wasn't enough.

God approached him with what became one of the most famous lines in the Bible—"Before I formed you in the womb I knew you" (Jeremiah 1:5 NIV). He had Jeremiah in mind for the role of prophet before Jeremiah's physical presence had even started to take shape.

"Before you were born I set you apart," the Lord said.

How do you argue against that?

A Real Long-Term Plan

Jeremiah's life was one of loneliness, frustration, and despair. But it wasn't in vain. His words and example lived on and inspired countless generations. God saw his life as more than just the years he lived. He saw the before, during, and after of Jeremiah's life.

Thankfully, most of us will never be called on to live such austere lives—but that doesn't mean He doesn't have a plan for us.

Before Jeremiah was conceived (in earthly terms), God knew what He wanted him to do. And the same will apply to each of us. We are not here by accident. Nothing in God's creation is accidental. So if you are here, God has a purpose behind that.

It need not be a history-shaping purpose like Jeremiah's, but who is to say that God values the example set by a godly parent any less than that set by a high priest? Who is to say that making a difference for the good in your neighborhood/team/family/workplace is valued any less than changing the course of a nation?

The difficult thing is determining what that purpose is. A more difficult thing might be accepting it once you understand what it is.

If it seems like too much or too little, if you think yourself overqualified or underqualified, just remember, this is what God had in mind for you all along. And you don't know the whole story. But He does.

The Answer to Jeremiah's Prayer

God doesn't always give us the easy way out. In fact, if He calls on us we can be sure there is some difficult work to be done.

God's answer to Jeremiah's claim that he is too young might be paraphrased as, "I made you for this. And with Me beside you, you are more ready than you could ever imagine!"

Jeremiah protests that he does not know how to speak. Presumably he means he does not know how to captivate a crowd or address the nobility. God answers this problem, as He does elsewhere with other men of faith, by putting His words into Jeremiah's mouth. He gives this youth authority "over nations and kingdoms to uproot and tear down, to destroy and overthrow, to build and to plant" (Jeremiah 1:10 NIV).

That's a big commission for a young boy, but Jeremiah accepts it. Israel and Judah, though, were famously stiff necked. Despite their long walk with God, they still refused to hear His Word. Jeremiah lived to see some serious uprooting and destroying when the armies of Babylon swept down from the north and God's people were taken into slavery and exile.

But the seeds he planted would grow in the hearts of the people until it was time to return home and begin anew.

Practical Prayers

- Dear Lord, if You forgive my initial hesitations, I will try to keep them as short as possible. I know You know better. You have always known better. But You know I have my fears, and they seem to be part of the human condition. So, understanding that, may we both work on washing those fears away with the cleansing effects of time, patience, and trust.

- Who am I, Father, to say what this life I am living is for? Did I create it? Will I dictate when it comes to a natural end? I am here because You willed it. You have a plan for me, and I can bring that to nothing, thanks to Your gift of free will, or I can gracefully and joyously fulfill it. Really, what I *should* do is thank You for making me a part of it!

- We read books and watch movies where individuals triumph against seemingly overwhelming odds, and it lifts our spirits. Why? Because we know, often without being consciously aware of it, that we are capable of greater things. The difference between fiction and real life is that we know who the power is that makes us capable of such things. It is You, Lord.

17

"I'M FINISHED, LORD, BUT LET ME DIE SHOWING YOUR ENEMIES YOUR POWER!"

A Prayer for Revenge

Then Samson prayed to the LORD, "Sovereign LORD, remember me. Please, God, strengthen me just once more, and let me with one blow get revenge on the Philistines for my two eyes." Then Samson reached toward the two central pillars on which the temple stood. Bracing himself against them, his right hand on the one and his left hand on the other, Samson said, "Let me die with the Philistines!"

JUDGES 16:28–30 NIV

Samson was a violent man in a violent time. Israel was an occupied land, and the Philistines were not kind masters. Perhaps God's people needed their judges to be men of action rather than philosophical souls.

He led the people for twenty years, and there must have been more to him than his feats of strength and his bad judgment when it came to women, but those are the stories we have.

Samson was one of that small group of individuals whose birth and prowess was foretold by an angelic visitation. Set aside as a Nazirite from before his birth, he was always meant to be a man of God, and the Lord seems to have gifted him with extraordinary strength. Unfortunately, he had the one weakness God warned His people against time and again. He had a penchant for pagan women, which he indulged to though it cost him dearly.

His marriage to a Philistine woman brought grief to himself and his people. His dalliance with a prostitute upset many. His love for Delilah was to be his undoing.

Perhaps he unconsciously sought his downfall because he relied more on women who couldn't be trusted than God, even to the point of providing one of them (who had already deceived him twice) with the secret of his strength.

Perhaps the physical cutting of his hair took away his strength, or perhaps God, in despair, had moved away from him. The effect was the same.

This once mighty warrior was blinded and made to toil in slavery. For special occasions, he was brought out and ridiculed. Of course, the Philistines weren't mocking him for having been a strong man, but for having been a representative of a god they didn't believe in. How powerful must the deity of the Israelites be if they could chain his man, beat him, and make him work like a beast of burden?

These things probably preyed on Samson's mind during his hours of captivity. He must have felt that his spiritual weakness had let God down. Now, with no hope of escape, he asked God to strengthen him for one last mighty act of revenge. The price he would extract for his eyes would also be a display of his God's power that thousands would see and many more would hear of.

They Take More Than They Give

Samson's story—or what we know of it—was full of selfish desire. He had a position of influence among his people and the power to back it up, but he used them largely to indulge what he saw as his needs.

That works, even today, but only for a while. Most of the earthly desires we indulge in eventually take more from us than they ever gave. None of them are ever for a greater good. And none of them last.

So we might be able to do those things because of what God has given us—money, beauty, athleticism, intelligence—but that doesn't mean we *should* do them. God never says, "Thou shalt not. . ." for His benefit. He says that because He knows the true cost of these things.

When you tell yourself, "I want to. . ." but then you decide it's better not to, not only do you not fall into the trap, but you become stronger spiritually. And, as if that isn't enough in itself, God usually rewards such obedience.

A life spent using God's gifts for God's ends need never end in revenge.

The Answer to Samson's Prayer

In response to his dying prayer, God gave Samson what he wanted most—strength! And Samson took his revenge.

Bracing himself against the pillars that held up the roof of the temple of Dagon, Samson pushed with all his God-given might. The pagan temple came crashing down on top of him, but it also killed thousands of Dagon worshippers and the leaders of the Philistines. So even in death he was a victorious leader of his people. The Philistines would have taken a long time to recover from the loss of their entire leadership and so many men. Israel would have been freed from the yoke of occupation for a while. Unfortunately, they chose to use the breathing space to fight among themselves.

A less obvious result was that Samson also freed himself from whatever "demon" led him on such a self-destructive path. In his last prayer, he acknowledged the Lord as sovereign and asked to be remembered by Him. Such an acknowledgment made daily, and throughout his life, might have brought his story to a different end, but his chosen end came and he would have been taken to his heavenly home afterward.

Practical Prayers

- Almighty God, the story of Samson reminds us that there is no place so low and so hopeless that You cannot reach us and set us free. You never forget us. We need only remember You.

- The talents and abilities You gave us, Lord, aren't toys and shouldn't be wasted. Sometimes I tell myself my gifts are small, but they are God-given; the more I use them as they are meant to be used, the more they will grow. The more they grow, the more work they do for You.

- Dear Lord, I know it! The temptations of this world are traps. They encourage me to be unworthy, then they convince me that I *am* unworthy. And the whole thing spirals down. I know it—but they still appeal to me. Help me, Lord, to understand who is talking to me at those times. And help me ignore him. Because I want to take the upward spiral.

18

"SWEET JESUS, I'VE WATCHED YOU. BUT CAN I DO AS YOU DID?"

A Prayer for the Lord's Power

But Peter put them all outside, and knelt down and prayed; and turning to the body he said, "Tabitha, arise." And she opened her eyes, and when she saw Peter she sat up. And he gave her his hand and raised her up. Then calling the saints and widows, he presented her alive. And it became known throughout all Joppa, and many believed in the Lord.

ACTS 9:40–42 ESV

The first martyr for the Christian faith, Stephen, had just been killed. The hunt was on for the rest of the disciples, and Saul of Tarsus was about to have his Damascus conversion. In the meantime, the disciples had scattered but hadn't stopped preaching.

As far as they were concerned, strengthened by the Holy Spirit, this was a time of miracles and wonders. Peter, once reckless and vainglorious, had been sobered by the reality of the power he now seemed to wear like a cloak. He had matured into a leader, but he was still learning as he went.

The days when he seemed to know everything were long gone. The fact that he was now performing the kind of miracles he had previously seen performed only by Jesus must have been pretty mind blowing for him. But he didn't forget where the power came from or in whose name he was doing these things.

In Lydda he told a bedridden man, "Jesus Christ heals you. Get up!" And the man got up. Word of this spread to Joppa, where Dorcas, or Tabitha, a good woman who was always helping others, had died. Her friends came to Lydda and set Peter his biggest challenge. Could he emulate his master in the greatest challenge of all, conquering death?

Peter seems to have approached the situation calmly enough. He went to the woman's bedside, then he sent everyone else out of the room. Then this powerful, famous man got onto his knees.

We do not know what words he used in his prayer, but we can imagine. Overcoming death was not something a man could do alone. This was the realm of Jesus Christ. So Peter humbled himself and, doubtless, invited his Lord into the room.

Then, with the lack of drama that implies absolute faith, and the lack of razzmatazz that speaks of simple reality, Peter said, "Tabitha, get up."

Did he doubt that he, a fisherman, could do this? The answer to that would be reflected in the answer to his prayer.

Life and How You Respond to It

Peter's situation here isn't so different from many we find ourselves in. Okay, we aren't expected to raise the dead, but time and again we find ourselves in overwhelming situations.

How do you usually respond when that happens? Do you panic, start micromanaging, call in your friends to help, call on your friends for distraction, plough ahead resigned to failure?

We talk and sing about being able to achieve anything through Christ who strengthens us, but all too often we rely on our own ability. We see it as our responsibility, and sometimes we manage and sometimes we don't.

Peter didn't see raising the dead woman as his work, so he probably felt no pressure to perform. This was Jesus' line of work. Peter simply had to hand it over.

The more we align how we live our lives with how God would have us live them, the more we can accept that our lives are God's work and the easier it becomes to hand our problems over to Him.

If our difficulties are ones we would have a problem handing over to the Lord, then they are probably difficulties we would be better off getting rid of.

The Answer to Peter's Prayer

Tabitha sat up!

Then Peter helped her to her feet.

A very simple but very effective answer. Peter then walked with her over to the window so that everyone waiting outside could see she lived. Perhaps Tabitha appreciated that she was still in her room while the others were outside. Coming back from the dead might have taken a moment or two to get used to.

The word spread, and many more people came to faith because of it. But they didn't come to faith because of Peter—they came to faith because Peter took himself out of the picture and allowed the Lord Jesus Christ in his place.

How Peter felt about having raised the dead isn't recorded. We are told he stayed at a nearby house "for some time." Perhaps he was preaching, or perhaps he was just getting his head around what had happened.

His experience of reality had just been greatly enlarged, and in Caesarea, God was already preparing a Roman centurion as the instrument for the next lesson.

Practical Prayers

- Dear Lord, when I am under pressure, may I remember to ask others to leave or find a quiet place for myself and invite You in. Lord, You and I can sort any problem out, so long as I make sure my entire contribution is letting You do the sorting out.

- Father God, may I never think I have all the answers. This life should be a learning process or there is no point to it. May I major in God and learn more about You every day.

- Lord, as I mature in my walk with You, may my works mature also. Even if I never perform anything the world might think of as a miracle, I will be content to see the miracles You work in me and the difference that makes to others I meet.

— 19 —
"ALMIGHTY GOD, WHY DO YOU BOTHER WITH ME?"

A Prayer of Humility and Awareness

Then King David went in and sat before the LORD, and he said: "Who am I, LORD God, and what is my family, that you have brought me this far? And as if this were not enough in your sight, my God, you have spoken about the future of the house of your servant. You, LORD God, have looked on me as though I were the most exalted of men. What more can David say to you for honoring your servant? For you know your servant."

1 CHRONICLES 17:16–18 NIV

In the full flush of his power, David might easily have thought of himself as a self-made man. After all, he had killed the giant who terrorized Saul's army; he had soothed the king with his harp playing; he had stayed loyal while running for his life; he had fought and won a war against his own son. It was no easy ride to the top and probably took all his resources.

He never fell into that trap. At every point, he praised God. He remembered where he came from.

If his father had been as successful as his great-grandfather, Boaz, then the family would be fairly well off, but David was the youngest of eight sons. When the others went to meet Samuel, he was left minding the livestock. Clearly, nothing much was expected of him.

But now God was assuring him that his lineage would be secure and would walk with the Lord even after his death. God told him his fame would live forever.

It must have been a sobering thought because David went to a quiet place of worship and said, in effect, "Okay, Lord. Why me?" This most powerful of men sat before his creator and pointed out that God was treating him as "a man of high degree" (1 Chronicles 17:17 KJV).

The prayer goes on to recount the things the Lord had already done and includes the fervent wish that His promises for the future be kept, not for David's family's sake but for the glory of God.

King David couldn't know it at that time, but the glory of God would be with his lineage intimately when the Lord came to earth in the form of David's direct descendant, Jesus Christ.

I Got Nothin'—But I Got Heart!

Many of us dream of positions of authority and influence—even if only at the neighborhood association or the local sports club. Some achieve that and more.

What stops the rest of us?

Well, sometimes it is lack of opportunity, but more often it is lack of belief in ourselves.

"Who am I?" we ask, "that anyone would listen to me?" "Who am I that I could actually make a difference for the better?" "Who am I that anyone would look beyond the neighborhood I live in and think I might have something to offer?"

In a world that seems only too keen to limit us, we limit ourselves.

David had seven brothers his father thought the high priest might like to meet. He wasn't even invited. And that must have been fairly standard behavior. So who would have figured the boy left behind would become one of the country's greatest leaders?

God did. Because God knew his heart.

The question we have to ask ourselves when thinking about achieving something is not "What kind of resources can I bring?" or "How can I get people's attention?" or "What do I stand to gain from this?" It should always be "What's in my heart for this?" and "Would God approve of what's in my heart?"

The Answer to David's Prayer

David's prayer was one of humility and thanks, not really requiring an answer.

But God did keep the promises that inspired it.

The verses in 1 Chronicles that follow David's prayer are a list of military victories and treasures dedicated to God. In one of these battles, his nephew followed his example and slayed a giant who taunted the Israelite army. Of course, David didn't make it easy for the Lord. He ordered a census of the armed forces that caused division, and tempted by Bathsheba's beauty, he stole her from her husband.

Who was he, indeed, that the Lord loved him? But his family went on, his fame endured, and people across the world know his story more than two-and-a-half-thousand years later. We know him for his faults, but most of all, we know him for his love of God. And God's love for him.

Practical Prayers

- Help me, Lord, to look down on no one, understanding that their position might have been mine without all You have done for me and that You might raise up any one of us at any time. Help me, Lord, to live such a life that I need not be ashamed to face anyone in heaven.

- Father God, may I never think I have done this on my own. May I always see the good as a gift and the difficult as a test—usually leading toward greater, and unexpected, gifts. Give me the strength and understanding to welcome both as You send them into my life.

- Who am I, Lord? I am a child of the Most High, which is at once a humbling thing and a glorious thought. If I am as nothing, it is with the understanding that everything You created is wonderful. If I am wonderful, it is only as a reflection of the one who created and redeemed me.

20

"I DON'T CARE IF MY COVER'S BLOWN. I KNOW WHO YOU ARE!"

A Prayer of Justified Fear

And there was in their synagogue a man with an unclean
spirit; and he cried out, saying, Let us alone; what have we
to do with thee, thou Jesus of Nazareth? Art thou come
to destroy us? I know thee who thou art, the Holy One of
God. And Jesus rebuked him, saying, Hold thy peace, and
come out of him. And when the unclean spirit had torn
him, and cried with a loud voice, he came out of him.

MARK 1:23–26 KJV

"What do you want from me?" Has anyone ever uttered those words in anything other than a spirit of fear?

The Gospel of Mark takes us straight to Jesus as a full-grown man about to begin His ministry. It tells us of John the Baptist, Jesus' baptism, the gathering of (some of) the disciples, and then it places Him squarely up against the establishment.

Jesus preached in the synagogue.

Now the synagogue was a place of faith, and no doubt good men gathered there encouraging each other to live good lives, but their teachings were firmly rooted in the past. Jesus was about to tell them that the kingdom of God was here!

He read from the scrolls not just as someone who knew the words but as someone who could explain to them, perhaps for the first time, the true meaning of the words. He read them as if He had lived them. And the people who heard were amazed.

But one, at least, was offended. If this man was, indeed, possessed by a demon, then perhaps he had put a lot of work into making those words just words. He may have subtly shifted the local community away from the spirit of the message until the scrolls themselves were revered more than the God they referred to.

Imagine how such a creature would have felt hearing the Word bring those words back to life!

He didn't hide who he was. He point-blank named Jesus as "the Holy One of God" and asked if He had come to destroy them. What kind of person would think that the Holy One would come to destroy them? An evil spirit? Or a human who has become something other than his Creator made him to be? In the last case, we might substitute "redeem" for "destroy."

What does God want from us? He wants better. That can be a scary prospect—but it's also a wonderful one!

The Problem Avoids the Cure

How would you tell an unclean spirit from someone who was simply obnoxious? I doubt you could. How would you tell a possessed person from someone lashing out because they had been hurt? I doubt there would be any point. The effects are the same. The answer is the same.

Jesus!

You might have someone in mind who fits the bill of a person possessed in such a way. Or there might be aspects of your life you simply have no control over. Remember, Jesus has the power to dismiss them and restore you.

Unfortunately, it isn't always as obvious as a demon jumping up and saying, "Here I am!" That man and the unclean spirit were known in that synagogue; they had probably been there for some time, may even have held a position of power, and subtly, over many years, have been robbing their church of any spiritual authenticity.

The demon who jumped up and shouted "I know you" wasn't being subtle, but usually their work is more difficult to identify. How do you detect it in others or in your own life? Well, it's any behavior that moves you further away from the cure for that behavior.

The Answer to the Unclean Spirit's Prayer

Jesus had stepped up. No longer a boy in Joseph's house, He had declared Himself before God and man at His baptism, and to the devil in the desert shortly afterward. All the "combatants" have been informed. The war had begun. And this was the first skirmish.

Jesus didn't quibble with the spirit. He didn't explain or reason. He told it to be quiet and leave the man alone. The spirit didn't go easily. Some versions of the Bible say it shook the man violently, others say it tore him. But it went. It did what it was told, and the same thing happened every time Jesus encountered one of these spirits.

These days, when some are not so keen on talking about unclean spirits, we have similar instances where people might be gripped by addictions or by hurts that twist their lives out of shape. Jesus can command them too.

As for the man in the synagogue who played host to this unclean spirit—what of him? How was he after the encounter? Shaken? Torn? But he was in the presence of a healing power that would not leave him so. We aren't told in this instance, but being set free in Christ is always a restorative event. Who knows how this experience shaped his life?

How would it shape yours?

Practical Prayers

- Lord, what do You want from me? To destroy me? Or to take away the parts of me that hold me back, the parts that imprison me and keep me from You? I know the answer, but part of me is scared by the thought. I'm comparing it to surgery that will remove a problem and leave me healthier. I'd be scared going in, but I would trust the surgeon. So, leaving my fear behind, I step up and say, "Lord, do what You will with me."

- What do You want from me, Almighty God? To love my neighbors, my enemies, and You. Love wants love from me. May I spend the rest of my life giving it.

- What do You want from me, Jesus, Son of God? To fully understand what You did for me and why. And to understand that You believed I was worth it. I'm trying, Jesus.

21

"GOD, I NEED YOU. BUT I CAN'T FIND YOU!"

A Prayer of Abandonment

Now from the sixth hour there was darkness over all the land until the ninth hour. And about the ninth hour Jesus cried out with a loud voice, saying, "Eli, Eli, lema sabachthani?" that is, "My God, my God, why have you forsaken me?"

MATTHEW 27:45–46 ESV

If you believe in God, you have to believe He is all in all. If ever you found yourself looking around and unable to find Him, then that would be a loneliness to put all other lonely feelings to shame.

That's where Jesus—who knew God better than anyone ever has—found Himself. His physical body was dying on a wooden cross. His divine nature would not have lessened that pain one bit. Pain would have messed with His thinking. The reasons why He was there, going through all this, might have been temporarily lost to Him. All the fears He expressed in His Gethsemane prayers would have been running riot in His head.

This man in His early thirties had been jailed, flogged, stripped, spat on; a crown of thorns had been pushed onto his head. They nailed Him to some wooden beams, hoisted Him none too gently into the air where His whole weight pulled against the spikes driven through His hands and feet. Then the guards, the people watching, the priests, the teachers, and even the men crucified with Him poured ridicule on Him.

The God of love—His Father—must have seemed very far away at that cruelly human moment.

Despite knowing this had to happen, He cried out in despair, looking for some comfort—and God stayed silent.

If God Taught You to Ride a Bike

Have you ever felt abandoned, with no one you could rely on? Have you ever felt like the only one trying to do a right thing in a wrong world?

Times like that are when people question the existence of God. It's a very lonely place to be. At times like that, you need someone who knows what you are going through. Of course, at times like that everyone suddenly seems to have their act spectacularly together. Jesus—uniquely of all the so-called gods humankind has worshipped—knew exactly what that felt like.

But He also knew that He had to go through that moment on His own for the greater good, despite the closeness, but seeming unavailability, of God.

But it can be a good thing too! Imagine a child learning to ride a bike. At a certain point the parent lets go of the seat and runs along behind the new young cyclist. The child isn't even aware of the parent anymore—although the parent is intensely aware of the child. All the child knows is that Mom or Dad isn't there anymore—and they are riding the bike!

It's a growing thing.

We know God isn't going to leave us just because we do a wrong or bad thing. But He might step back (or run along behind us) while we take that feeling of abandonment, understand it, and help someone else feeling the same way, or while we become the reliable one for someone else, or stand up—on our own—for a right thing in a wrong world.

Did God abandon Jesus? Definitely not. Has He ever abandoned you? No—but He may have stood back and watched while you did what He sent you there to do.

The Answer to Jesus' Prayer

Nothing worth achieving is ever cheaply bought, and for our salvation God sacrificed Himself. How could He answer anyone at that moment when He was fully absorbed in the death of Jesus—in dying Himself? Is it any wonder that as Jesus was crying out, as it says in the Gospel of Mark, "darkness came over all the land"? God was giving Himself up to death.

Jesus, when not in agony, would never have expected an answer—would never have imagined God was not right there with Him. And He would have been right. God was there. He was so fully engaged there was nothing left to say.

In answer to Jesus' prayer God may have wept, but He didn't interfere. He didn't respond to the all-too-human cry of weakness. He understood it was an important part of what was happening, because if Jesus did not experience every aspect of humanity, how could He then be there for us in our troubles?

What else might He have done? Saved His Son? And lost the rest of us. Weighing that dilemma brings it home just how much was sacrificed for us.

In this instance, as difficult as it might be to imagine and as terrible as it must have been to experience, God's silence was the perfect reply to prayer.

Practical Prayers

- Almighty God, I learn from You every way I can—from Your words in the Bible, from the prompting of the Holy Spirit, from the examples of men and woman who have walked with You throughout history. Help me also to learn from Your silence and to understand what it is You are really saying when You don't say anything.

- Beloved Jesus, I forget. I forget—or take for granted—just how much You went through for me. It is a comfort—when I dare to think about it—that there is no spiritual or emotional place I can go where You can not only rescue me but will already be there waiting for me when I arrive.

- So, God, I have to do this by myself. Is that what You are telling me? Is that why You have gone quiet? Well. . .thank You for the faith You have in me. You put me here for a reason; now let me repay Your trust. Just forgive me, Lord, if I wobble a little. I won't fall off. You wouldn't have let go of me if that was going to happen!

22

"GOD, GIVE ME THE FAITH OF A CHILD."

A Prayer of Thanks for Simplicity

At that time Jesus declared, "I thank you, Father, Lord of heaven and earth, that you have hidden these things from the wise and understanding and revealed them to little children; yes, Father, for such was your gracious will."

MATTHEW 11:25–26 ESV

In science-fiction movies and even an episode of *The Big Bang Theory*, scientists put a lot of effort into devising a means of communicating with alien life forms.

Well, as Jesus was teaching and preaching in the towns of Galilee, we are told that God did something like that. He sent a message anyone can understand. As it says in the book of Jeremiah, God wrote His laws in people's hearts using the finger of the Spirit.

Sure, He wrote them in everyone's hearts, but not everyone can read them. As people grow, they accumulate desires, resentments, ambitions; these earthy things cover the message up until we all but forget it exists—until it becomes nothing more than a little voice whispering beneath the noise of our busy minds.

God's truths are simple ones. Love God. Love one another. You would think we, as sensible, mature adults, couldn't complicate those instructions. And yet we do. People will tie themselves into theological knots trying to justify not loving that neighbor or killing that enemy.

By the time we are a grown-up in this world, we are—unless we're spiritually enlightened by words like these—a mass of distractions. And some might say the world does that to us deliberately to keep us from hearing that little voice.

Jesus was more than a little frustrated that the cities He had visited recently and performed miracles in had not followed Him in the way He hoped. Those busy, cosmopolitan city dwellers probably thought themselves too sophisticated for miracles.

But, even while being frustrated by the so-called intelligentsia, Jesus gave thanks for their lack of understanding. Because with hearts and minds such as theirs, the kingdom of heaven would never be for them. First, they had to shed those notions of their own importance, accept that they did not—and could not—know it all, and understand that they couldn't do this life thing on their own strength.

They needed to become as little children again, as He says in Matthew 18:3, if they were to have any hope of heaven.

Childlike, Not Child-ish

"So. . .if I become more childlike, won't the world just take advantage of me?"

"It doesn't matter. This world ends."

"And, you're saying that I could spend my life trying to know more and more about the universe and my part in it, but it might be for nothing?"

"Yup. Because there is no end to figure out. But trusting and having faith are very short journeys. So short, in fact, that children make them all the time."

Imagine there really is a Creator (if you didn't already believe). How would a creation of His be able to comprehend Him without actually coming close to being Him? How much respect would a Creator be worth if we could come to terms with Him intellectually?

Understanding was never going to be the way to go.

But a life spent in trust and wonder? That's a whole different prospect and more like we might expect from a God worthy of the name.

Try it for a while in this life and see how it works. Step out in innocence and love. Sure, the world will knock you down—but wonder will lift you back up! Admit to not knowing the answers, but commit to fully exploring the question. Be dependable, but depend on God rather than yourself.

The rewards will be nothing like you ever expected, but they will be better in ways you don't quite understand.

A childlike—but not childish—life is a little bit of heaven on earth. Good practice for when we are all children in the eternal home of our Father.

The Answer to Jesus' Prayer

The answer to Jesus' prayer in this instance is the possibility of salvation for all. After all, everyone, no matter what else they might turn out to be in later life, has been a child.

The understanding of things beyond comprehension, the being comfortable with the unknowable, the simple assurance of love (or the knowledge that if they aren't loved then they ought to be)— they are all there in the heart of the child who became the adult.

It isn't easy to go backward, to unlearn all we thought was important, to trust our deepest feelings of belonging. But it is possible. And it's not like we have to figure it out for ourselves. It's right there in the Bible.

Of course, some will always rely on their own understanding, on their man-made empires of intellect. And Jesus also warned that Capernaum's fate would be no different from Sodom's if the people living there did not repent and seek those laws they carried around with them in their hearts, apparently unaware.

Both the explanation and the warning still apply today.

Practical Prayers

- Lord, You would have us be as a child. And You also tell us pride is a sin. Is it a coincidence that the second one tries so hard to keep me from being the first? I don't think so. The quicker I jettison the pride and learn to live in trust the better.

- Almighty God, all our science and study tells us a lot about *how* things happen but nothing about *why* they happen. For most children, *why* is a favorite and perhaps overused word. May I be able to respond to the why, why, whys of the world in a childlike fashion by answering always, "God, God, God."

- We don't have the answers, dear Lord. We prove that by the mess we make of Your world. Understanding is always too far away to reach. But the leap of faith is a short one. On the other side, we see our old questions didn't need answers, and there are answers to questions we never thought to ask. It's a place of childlike wonder, so it's no surprise that You want us to be children before we come in.

23

"LORD, EVEN IF I DIE WRAPPED IN SEAWEED, MAY MY LAST WORDS PRAISE YOU."

A Prayer of Thanks in Extremity

"When my life was ebbing away, I remembered you, Lord, and my prayer rose to you, to your holy temple. Those who cling to worthless idols turn away from God's love for them. But I, with shouts of grateful praise, will sacrifice to you. What I have vowed I will make good. I will say, 'Salvation comes from the Lord.'" And the Lord commanded the fish, and it vomited Jonah onto dry land.

JONAH 2:7–10 NIV

Jonah was a prophet. But he was a bit of a grumpy, unwilling prophet. Why? Well, because the God he served kept giving people second chances. Jonah probably wanted a bit more fire and brimstone. Like the old days!

So when God asked him to take a message to Nineveh, Jonah declined. Not because Nineveh was the capital city of Israel's greatest enemy, Assyria. Not because he might be in grave personal danger. No. He declined to go because he knew the Ninevites would repent and God would forgive them.

Part of the problem was that he believed such repentance would be short lived and therefore not worthwhile.

So he ran away. He surely didn't think he could hide from God, but perhaps he thought that if he traveled far enough in the wrong direction God would ask someone else to go to Nineveh.

He booked passage on a boat heading for Tarshish. But God didn't change His mind. God brought a storm so fierce that experienced sailors feared for their lives and prayed to every god they had ever heard of to save them.

At this point, Jonah seems to have accepted the inevitable—just not God's idea of the inevitable. Deciding his life was forfeit, he asked the sailors to save themselves by throwing him overboard. He probably expected to drown. And it must have been close. In his prayer, he describes sinking down to the roots of the mountains and his life ebbing away. There is no hint of surprise at being swallowed whole by a giant fish and being able to breathe—and pray—again.

He had, of course, known God a long time and must have been used to His wonders and His ways. But it takes a very cool customer to pray from the belly of a fish and not be surprised to find himself there.

It also takes an amazing God to use not only the sea but the creatures living in it to have His will be done!

The Destination Is Sometimes the Excuse for the Journey

God doesn't need you!

Let me rephrase that. God loves you, wants to spend eternity with you, and would miss you if you weren't there—but He doesn't need you. If God wants to get something done, He can do it all by Himself. What couldn't God do?

So if God wants you to do something for Him, you better believe there is something in it for you.

The book of Jonah ends rather abruptly with God still trying to explain mercy and compassion to the wayward prophet. We don't know if he finally comes to understand the beauty of the lesson, but it's hard to imagine God going to all that effort and the point not being made. Hopefully, Jonah was a better man and prophet for the experience and the (eventual) understanding.

If God calls you to do something, sure, there will be an earthly point to it. Wounds might be healed, people might be helped. But you will go on a journey. It will be a growing and learning experience for you. Parts of you that you didn't know were broken may be restored. Experience gained and pain suffered will prove to be of benefit further down the road in ways you couldn't have imagined.

When God calls you to do something, the journey will be every bit as important as the destination. How long that journey is depends on whether you run toward Him. . .or away from Him.

The Answer to Jonah's Prayer

The rest of the story is less about the answer to Jonah's prayer than it is about the continuation of God's work.

As he was dying, Jonah remembered the Lord; he understood better than ever that no earthly treasures or idols could take His place, and that his life was God's to do with as He would. Amid that deep-sea sense of peace and acceptance, God scooped Jonah up—via a giant fish—and saved his life.

Three probably very smelly days later, the fish vomited him out onto the shore. We can only imagine those three days of travel had taken him back in the direction of Nineveh, where God wanted him to be.

Jonah preached, the Ninevites repented (for the most part, temporarily), and God spared the city. Then Jonah grumbled, saying in effect, "This is what I said would happen. What a waste of time!"

But let's look at the situation again. The Ninevites disobeyed God, Jonah preached, they repented, God didn't destroy them, and eventually many of them went back to their old ways. Jonah disobeyed God, he repented, God didn't destroy him, and eventually he went back to his old grumbling ways. Perhaps the Ninevites weren't the only ones who should have been glad our God is a God of second chances.

Practical Prayers

- Lord, I don't know. That's all. I don't know. As much as I think I understand, You know infinitely more. So when I start to object to or grumble about how You want to work things out, have pity on me. And have patience. I'll get there.

- Almighty Father, I imagine a book somewhere in heaven with all the answers to the questions of my life. And I expect to be astounded when I read it. Until then, may I make the answer to all my questions "Thy will be done."

- Dear God, even in the midst of Jonah's rebellion You found new followers among the sailors. I am in constant awe that You can work even human frailty and disobedience into Your all-encompassing plan. May my embarrassing mistakes also be used for Your glory.

24

"GOD, I'M TELLING THE TRUTH. AND IF I'M NOT, YOU KNOW!"

A Prayer That God Examine a Heart

Hear me, LORD, my plea is just; listen to my cry. Hear my prayer—it does not rise from deceitful lips. Let my vindication come from you; may your eyes see what is right. Though you probe my heart, though you examine me at night and test me, you will find that I have planned no evil; my mouth has not transgressed.

PSALM 17:1–3 NIV

David was being hunted!

Psalm 17 is part of a collection of the words and prayers of King David. As such, there is no proper setting for this prayer, but we can guess from the words that he was calling out to God from a hiding place while his enemies gathered around him.

From his confidence in not having strayed from the Lord's path we might guess he was still a young man. It is suggested elsewhere that this prayer was uttered as Saul searched for him. He might have offered a similar prayer during the war with his son, Absalom.

The younger David would have had more confidence in asking the Lord to probe his heart and examine his words. Of course, the older man understood that God was very familiar with the workings of his heart and his mouth.

In this instance, whenever it was, David draws a distinction between himself as a follower of God's teaching and his enemies as men who have closed their hearts to the divine and seek earthly rewards instead. He asks God to raise him up and to confound the enemy forces.

God, of course, is aware of the whole situation and doesn't really need the reminder. But sometimes we say these prayers as much to remind ourselves as anything.

We take a big chance when we ask God to check our words and look into our hearts. But, in this case, even though David wasn't too confident of his own survival, he was confident that he was in God's hands and had walked a godly path to his current hiding place.

So he was justified in asking God to lead him safely out of it again.

I Hope God Didn't See *That*

We know that God knows everything and sees everything. Well, intellectually we know it. But how much we actually believe it will help shape our lives.

King David petitioned God, reminding Him that he had walked in His ways to get to where he was. As a challenge or a plea, he asked God to examine his heart and see if he was lying.

Wow! How many of us would take that chance? Most of us have passwords on our phones and computers just so our innermost thoughts can't be accessed by anyone else. How comfortable would we be presenting anyone with the password to our heart?

The thing is, God made that heart. He doesn't need a password. He already knows what lives in there. Understanding that God truly is everywhere—even there—ought to have some effect on us. Some will try and hide the thoughts they don't want seen, others will try to deny them. Neither of those options even makes sense.

The only way to go—understanding that not only does God know our truths and lies right now but that we will one day have to answer for them face-to-face—is to bring our heart and our words into line with God's will.

It sounds a little like giving away our individuality. In reality, it is more like becoming the beautiful person and living the wonderful life God always had planned for you.

The Answer to David's Prayer

Psalm 18 is a celebratory piece set to music, in which King David gives thanks to God for delivering him from all his enemies, in particular from the hands of Saul. It could be taken as his response to God's reply to his earlier prayer.

He tells of how "the cords of death" entangled him and "the torrents of destruction" overwhelmed him (Psalm 18:4). And yet, if we look back to the prayer spoken from his hiding place, he seems pretty cool and trusting about it all. That's faith!

So God delivered him and raised him up. The Creator and the king enjoyed a special relationship in which God always knew the heart of David. Even when Samuel was looking among David's brothers for a future king, the Lord told him He was looking at their hearts. Later in life when David gave in to temptation, the Lord knew what was in his heart and sent Nathan to rebuke him. David was humbled and resumed his walk with God.

In his prayer, David resolved that his words would not be sinful and he would live by the Lord's words. And so we find that both sets of words are still here for us to examine and learn from.

Practical Prayers

- Beloved Father, I could make all kinds of excuses, and I do: to my wife, my work colleagues, myself. But You know they are excuses and also know the fears and insecurities that cause them. It's embarrassingly intimate. But the fact that You know me in that way and still stick around tells me I can rely on You like no other. And I can do better, for You.

- Dear Lord, when I lie, when I cut corners, when I avoid doing the right thing, choosing instead the easy thing, I pretend that's not what I'm doing—but part of me always knows. And my soul shrivels a little more each time I do it. Now I have to ask, who benefits from that? Lord, I will not give the other side any more of me. Lift me up above the traps of this world and restore my beleaguered soul.

- Come, Jesus. This hovel is my heart. It's not what the people who know me would expect. I would be ashamed to show it to them. But I am showing it to You. And asking You to live there with me as together we do a beautiful work of restoration.

— 25 —
"YOUR PRAYERS TELL ME YOU'RE THE MAN FOR THIS MISSION."

A Prayer as a Memorial Offering

About the ninth hour of the day he clearly saw in a vision an angel of God who had just come in and said to him, "Cornelius!" And fixing his gaze on him and being much alarmed, he said, "What is it, Lord?" And he said to him, "Your prayers and alms have ascended as a memorial before God. Now dispatch some men to Joppa and send for a man named Simon, who is also called Peter."

ACTS 10:3–5 NASB

Cornelius was a foreigner among a people who had been warned not to mix with foreigners for centuries. Worse than that, he was part of an occupying army!

Despite all that, he was respected by the Jews who knew him; he and his family worshipped God, and he helped the needy in his local community. He may or may not have been the same centurion who petitioned Jesus to heal his servant.

He was a man whose faith could be read in the way he lived his life. He gave with no expectation of receiving, and he prayed with no notion that his prayers would earn him a visit from an angelic messenger.

But they did!

An angel appeared and told him God had taken notice of his prayers and good deeds. The reward for those things was not something material for himself (in the short term); rather, he was trusted to carry out another work for God. No explanation was given. He was simply told to send for Simon who was called Peter at the house of Simon the tanner in Joppa.

The fact the angel gave both of Peter's names might even suggest that Cornelius didn't know the fisherman. Even if he had heard of him, he didn't know that Peter was about to experience a transformative vision of his own and the two events would be connected.

If Cornelius was the centurion who asked Jesus to heal his servant, then that same servant may well have been the "devout soldier" who was his assistant and one of the ones sent to Joppa.

So Cornelius sent for a man he didn't know, asking him to come to his house in contravention of Jewish laws, for a purpose he was unaware of—and this invitation may even have gotten him into trouble with his military superiors. Obviously God needed a man of considerable faith to do such a thing!

Whatever God Wants, Whenever He Wants It

One of the worst things that can happen to a person's faith is for it to become a matter of routine. Not that there aren't practices that should be habitual, but when we believe that this action always brings that response and things continue forever in the same routine, then we are, perhaps, missing something.

God, as we see time and again in the Bible, has a habit of upsetting people's routines to get His work done. People don't always respond positively to that.

Cornelius did. Perhaps the heart he put into his prayers and the selfless ways he helped others convinced the Lord that this was a man He could use for a good cause.

Faith at its best and most useful is always open to the will of God. And as no man or woman can predict God's will, we have to be open to a myriad of possibilities—always assuming they come from God.

The Answer to Cornelius' Prayer

Simon Peter, the disciple/apostle, was in the midst of a transformative period of his life. Jesus, his master, had ascended to heaven, and now Peter, not previously noted for his organizational skills, had been left in charge. He was healing people in Jesus' name and had just had a vision that turned his ideas of purity on their head.

Then this Gentile, Cornelius, sent for him.

Standing in the house of a foreigner with other Jews and Gentiles, which his previous idea of religion would have forbidden him to do, Peter listened as Cornelius explained how an angel had told him to send for Simon known as Peter—and even told him the address where Peter could be found. Then Cornelius asked Peter to tell them all what God had disclosed to him.

Peter did so, and the Holy Spirit, in a sort of second Pentecost, filled the room and affected everyone in it, Jew and Gentile.

The baptism of Cornelius and his family represented the inclusion of the rest of the world in the Good News. Faith and salvation were no longer the sole right of the Jewish people. An Italian soldier and a Galilean fisherman brought the world together in the name of Jesus Christ.

Practical Prayers

- Being a man of God in an army of occupation could not have been a comfortable position to be in. May I, Lord, always shine Your light, regardless of the company around me.

- Lord, it's an easy thing to promise when it isn't actually being asked of you, but may I have the courage and love to go where You tell me when You tell me, trusting the explanation will come in Your good time.

- Beloved Father, the coming together of Jew and Gentile reminds me that Your love is for everyone. May I be like Cornelius and reach out in faith, or be like Peter and go where I'm not "supposed" to—all to be an instrument of Your love.

26

"GOD. . .HAVE YOU HAD ENOUGH OF BEING ANGRY YET?"

A Prayer for Undeserved Mercy

In the first year of Darius the son of Ahasuerus, of Median descent, who was made king over the kingdom of the Chaldeans—in the first year of his reign, I, Daniel, observed in the books the number of the years which was revealed as the word of the LORD to Jeremiah the prophet for the completion of the desolations of Jerusalem, namely, seventy years. So I gave my attention to the Lord God to seek Him by prayer and supplications, with fasting, sackcloth and ashes.

DANIEL 9:1–3 NASB

The book of Daniel might easily be split into two books. The first half has lions and fiery ovens—the second half has the apocalypse!

The first half tells the stories of a group of young Hebrew noblemen, Daniel and his friends, who steadfastly maintained their faith even in the palace of their pagan captors. The second half contains the visions and prayers of Daniel.

In this prayer, Daniel took responsibility for his nation.

Is that even possible? Can one man of faith take responsibility for an entire people? Yet there are several examples in the Bible.

Daniel agreed with the Lord that the Judeans and Israelites behaved terribly, despite warnings, and that their dispersal into slavery and destitution was really the only option He had left. Daniel acknowledged that the point of their near destruction as a nation was that they might learn, and he agreed that, for the most part, they hadn't learned.

But! Looking at the words of Jeremiah, who predicted just such a fall, Daniel saw that the anger of the Lord has a limited term. And perhaps the time was up.

By this point in the story, no one could doubt Daniel's courage or his faith. He had stayed true to the Lord under threat of being eaten by lions. His faith was such that angels intervened on his behalf. But what kind of relationship did he have with God that he could petition heaven, saying something like, "You were right to punish us, Lord, and we still haven't learned our lesson— but You are better than this"?

The undeserved mercy Daniel prayed for, the new beginning, the opportunity to be "born again" as a nation, is something that would come to completeness in the form of Jesus Christ. But just because His mercy hadn't come into the world in a physical form at that time didn't mean it wasn't always an aspect of God. It was. And Daniel was counting on it!

Ashes? With *My* Complexion?

Fasting. Sackcloth. Ashes. At times, these seem to be the uniform that must be worn to approach the Lord.

But how many of us have sackcloth in our linen closet?

As usual, it is not the *things* that matter but what they stand for and what is done with them. Daniel, we know from his book, lived in a palace (albeit unwillingly) and had access to the best of foods. His clothes would have been quality garments, and his skin and hair would have been cleaned with fine oils and lotions.

What right would he have to pray against that sort of society while he still indulged in its luxuries? How could he pray for the restoration of a people generally reduced to poverty while living the lifestyle of their oppressors?

Likewise, God might look askance at us if we prayed for this country to be a more godly one while we indulge ourselves in aspects of it that might have to be swept away to make that prayer come to fruition.

While still living in Babylon, Daniel turned his back on what it had to offer as an example of his sincerity as he approached his Lord. God listened and responded.

One man or woman of faith can intercede for a family, a town, a people. And if enough people turned their backs on the things that were not of God, we might find something like the kingdom of heaven established here sooner than we expected.

The Answer to Daniel's Prayer

Daniel's prayer came to fruition some decades later when Artaxerxes decided, for no apparent reason, to release them. Not only did he release the people, he restored their precious artifacts and gave them supplies to rebuild their temple.

Now what would possess a ruler to do such things?

But there was also a more immediate response (which helps explain the delay). Daniel, who may have had more heavenly visitors than anyone in the Bible, was approached by yet another angel!

The messenger of the Lord told him that the time of punishment was indeed fixed, but the time of restoration wasn't quite there yet.

More than that, the angel told Daniel of the fixed time periods to come, including the one where the Anointed One (Jesus Christ) would be cut down, and the time when an abomination would rise up and lay waste to the world until the end that was decreed (the lake of fire from Revelation) came down upon him.

107

In "reminding" God of His fixed terms, and through his faith, Daniel was given a vision of all God's fixed terms, right up until the very end, showing that God has the beginning, the end, and everything in between firmly in His hands.

Practical Prayers

- Almighty God, may I never think one person can't make a difference when that one person is a creation of Yours.

- Lord, before I come to You in prayer, may I examine myself and my own life, making sure it is pleasing to You before I ask You to change anything else.

- Our Father, when I come to You in prayer, may I learn not to worry about whether You will grant my request or not; rather, may I only wonder how much more You will provide if only I ask in faith, love, and trust.

27

"FATHER, DON'T TAKE THEM HOME. BUT WALK BESIDE THEM INTO THE BATTLE!"

A Prayer for the Ones Left Behind

"I have given them your word and the world has hated them, for they are not of the world any more than I am of the world. My prayer is not that you take them out of the world but that you protect them from the evil one. They are not of the world, even as I am not of it."

JOHN 17:14–16 NIV

Jesus spoke more clearly to the disciples than ever before—and it scared them!

They were in the upper room, the Last Supper finished. Judas had gone. The remaining eleven were thoroughly confused, and there was no time left for anything other than straight talk.

Despite them having just entered the city to shouts of *Hosanna* and there being no obvious immediate threat, Jesus told the shocked disciples they would soon have to get by without Him. Not only that, but the world would hate them as it hated Him.

However, He promised them they would not be left alone. And we can only wonder how comforting the thought of this new thing, the Holy Spirit, was to men in real physical danger—an invisible comforter against angry priests and a merciless Roman governor.

He told them they would weep and mourn—but their grief would turn to joy. He told them they would be hiding in their homes and He would be left alone.

We can only wonder how many of them felt like going home at that point.

Then, amid the confusion, Jesus turned His face heavenward.

He told His Father the time had arrived and He was coming home. He gave thanks for the ones God prepared for Him and said that now He had "uncovered" them and made them "not of the world," through the word of God He was going to leave them behind.

At this point, they probably wished God would take them to heaven with their Lord. But there was work for them to do. They had to stay behind. Jesus had one request of His Father—it was not that He strengthen them against the powers of the world, but that He protect them from the evil one.

If nothing else, that prayer must have brought it home to the disciples who it really was they were up against.

Choose *His* Battles

There are battles to be fought in this world, but we have to wonder—how many of them should be of interest to Christians? We aren't called on to depose tyrants or defeat armies. Judas seems to have expected Jesus to care about such things—but He didn't.

The mission He left His disciples was to proclaim the kingdom of God and to love each other. James, the half brother of Jesus and leader of the church in Jerusalem, defined true religion as caring for widows and orphans.

That's all good stuff. That's wonderful stuff. So why does the world fight so hard against it? Because there is a bigger battle going on. A battle fought on a higher level than earthly politics and power plays, fought using the details of ordinary life.

If we read the book of Revelation, we see that Jesus and the Father have the higher battle well in hand, but meanwhile we are down here fighting the evil one on our own with. . .what. . .love? Really?

First, love, even in the smallest details of an ordinary life, is more powerful than we can imagine. And second, we are no more alone than the disciples were after Pentecost. The Holy Spirit is with those who have made themselves "not of the world" by declaring their allegiance to a better world.

But if we want to have the Holy Spirit on our side, we have to choose our battles wisely. The clue to making the right choice is that they have to be fought in love.

The Answer to Jesus' Prayer

The disciples *did* scatter and hide. They *were* afraid. Judas sold Jesus. Peter denied Him. Christ was crucified, and they were left alone. If Jesus hadn't changed the vengeful mind of Saul of Tarsus, they might have met the same fate as Stephen, the first Christian martyr.

But even the most cynical of observers would have to agree *something* happened to these men at Pentecost. This, more than anything, was God's answer to Jesus' prayer. The third aspect of the Trinity joined the battle.

The Comforter, or Companion, Jesus promised arrived in spectacular style. There were tongues of fire and the disciples were suddenly able to speak in many different languages. This scared, leaderless bunch who was prone to squabbling among themselves now become a force to be reckoned with—a church that would not only survive but spread to every corner of the world.

All but one of the men Jesus said would leave Him alone in His time of direst trouble went on to live and die as martyrs for His message. The remaining one, John, simply lived and died for it.

This invisible helper Jesus had promised them proved to be a more effective ally against the evil one than any of them could have imagined.

Practical Prayers

- Almighty God, the Holy Spirit was sent to expose the guilt of the world. I am guilty. But You know that. And You have already taken care of it. For that, and for Your Son, Lord, I would spend this life and beyond thanking You.

- Oh, there have been so many times I felt alone, Lord Jesus. So many! Until I came to understand I never really was alone, I just didn't want to hear what the Comforter had to say. For His presence and the words of God He speaks, I am grateful. Just teach me to listen a little better, Lord.

- God the Father, You have appeared and acted in awesome power. Lord Jesus, Your miracles were beyond the understanding of men. But the Holy Spirit works quietly, gently, dealing only in truth, conviction, and the Word of God. Now *there* is an example I can aspire to follow.

28

"THIS GOOD WOMAN TRUSTED US. MAY HER TRUST PROVE WELL FOUNDED!"

A Prayer for Deserved Rewards

Boaz replied to her, "All that you have done for your mother-in-law after the death of your husband has been fully reported to me, and how you left your father and your mother and the land of your birth, and came to a people that you did not previously know. May the LORD reward your work, and your wages be full from the LORD, the God of Israel, under whose wings you have come to seek refuge."

RUTH 2:11–12 NASB

Ruth took her marriage vows seriously!

When her husband, Mahlon, died she could have moved back in with her own family. She was young enough to begin again. But when her widowed mother-in-law, Naomi, decided to make the long journey back to her family home in Bethlehem, Ruth went with her.

Why? Naomi had nothing to offer her and nothing to sustain them but a small piece of land. It would mean setting up a home in a town where she knew no one and had no support system. But it was the position she would have held had her husband still been alive.

Ruth and Naomi arrived in Bethlehem at harvest time. Because they had nothing, Ruth offered to go "gleaning." In other words, she would ask permission to follow behind the harvesters, picking up any grain that fell to the ground. From these scraps she might be able to make a meal for her mother-in-law and herself. It was an occupation generally reserved for the poorest of the poor and seen as an offering to God by the farmers who allowed it. It would have been laborious work, requiring a fair degree of humility. A woman with no friends might have expected harassment from the farmhands or even the other gleaners.

Boaz, a kinsman of Naomi, happened to own the field Ruth was gleaning in. He had heard of this young foreign woman's love for her mother-in-law, and now he could see her dedication. Impressed, he told her only to glean in his field and he would see she was looked after, and she could share in the water his servants drank.

Then, addressing Ruth but calling on God, he prayed she would be justly rewarded and the land in which she had sought refuge would be a good home for her.

Tired, hungry, and overwhelmed at this unexpected kindness, Ruth asks a question many others have asked since, "Why have I found such favor in your eyes that you notice me—a foreigner?" (Ruth 2:10 NIV).

Whose Prayer Are We Working on Today, Lord?

Do you know the joke about the man who takes God to task, demanding to know why He doesn't do something about poverty, injustice, and war?

God looks down from on high and says, "I've been meaning to ask you the same thing."

It's not a joke!

If we are followers of Jesus, children of God, we will often find ourselves acting as the tools that implement His reply to prayer.

Our actions might be the answer to the prayer of someone we have never met, the response to a prayer we know nothing about.

But when it comes to our own prayers, we might stop on occasion and wonder, "Do I really need the power that oversees the universe to take care of this, or is this maybe something I could do myself. . .just to help Him along a little?"

If we are children of God but still expect Him to do all the work, then we are lazy, ungrateful children, and He might be justified in sending us some cosmic discipline.

If you live your life with the intention of being the answer to as many prayers as possible, you will be surprised how many prayers of your own are taken care of along the way.

The Answer to Boaz's Prayer

Boaz is the answer to Boaz's prayer.

Well, the man himself and everything God did to put him in the position where he could help.

His kindness caused Naomi to wonder if he might act as kinsman-redeemer to them. Because Boaz was related to her and her dead son, tradition would allow him to put forward a case for marrying Ruth. An honorable man, his interest doesn't seem to have extended beyond kindness, so Naomi urged Ruth to be a little more forward.

Even after waking up and finding Ruth keeping his feet warm, Boaz still didn't make a move. It seems another man had a closer kinsman-redeemer claim.

Rather than offer Ruth to this other man, Boaz called a meeting and said Naomi wanted to sell a small piece of land that belonged to her deceased son. The other man agreed to buy it. Then Boaz informed him that a wife came with the land. Tradition demanded that if he took this wife then their children would officially be of the lineage of her dead husband.

It was too much. He backed out.

As next kinsman in line, Boaz bought the land and married Ruth.

The book ends with Naomi cradling a newborn grandson, Obed, the grandfather of King David and great, great, great grandfather of Jesus.

Practical Prayers

- Lord, You have done so much for me and I don't know how I could repay You, but if I can lighten Your load even a little by answering a prayer or two for You, well, You know where I am.

- Father of all, who am I to look down on anyone because of their station in life, or their nationality, or any other thing? I see them in the present moment, You see the role they play in eternity. May my part in Your incredible plan always be one of offering a helping hand. What result might come of that I shall leave entirely up to You.

- In being hospitable to strangers, dear Lord, You remind us we might be entertaining angels, or an ancestor of Jesus, or. . .who knows? Remind us, Lord, that none are strangers in Your eyes.

29

"FATHER, YOU HEAR ME. I DON'T NEED TO SPEAK. BUT SOME NEED TO LISTEN."

A Prayer as a Lesson

Jesus said to her, "Did I not say to you that if you believe, you will see the glory of God?" So they removed the stone. Then Jesus raised His eyes, and said, "Father, I thank You that You have heard Me. I knew that You always hear Me; but because of the people standing around I said it, so that they may believe that You sent Me." When He had said these things, He cried out with a loud voice, "Lazarus, come forth."

JOHN 11:40–43 NASB

Israel in the time of Jesus had plenty of wonder-workers. They traveled from town to town, made a big production of their tricks, and took up a collection afterward.

Some have tried to paint Jesus as just another traveling wonder-worker, who, unfortunately, got crucified.

Not so.

People came to Him, asking for what became known as His miracles. Usually they were performed with the minimum of fuss: the instruction to get up, rubbing eyes, laying a hand on someone.

In this instance, though, Jesus might be said to have indulged in a little theatricality. But if that's what He was doing, there was a purpose to it.

Lazarus was dying. His sisters, Martha and Mary, who knew Jesus, sent word to Him in the hope He would heal their brother.

It is recorded that Jesus loved Martha and Mary. They might have expected Him to rush to their aid. But Jesus waited.

He had recently been stoned out of Judea where Lazarus lived, but that wasn't why He delayed going back. When He finally decided it was time to go, He went without hesitation. His disciples thought they were following Him to their deaths.

It was too late by the time He arrived (in worldly terms). Lazarus had been dead for four days. To be blunt, his corpse was already starting to smell.

This was all part of the show. No other wonder-worker could have rectified this situation.

Martha and Mary were distraught, but they expected to see their brother again after the resurrection. Jesus told them, "I am the resurrection," (John 11:25 NASB) and before a crowd of people—some of whom may have recently stoned Him—He walked up to Lazarus's tomb and prayed.

Then He stood in front of the tomb of a man who had spent four days in death and told him to come back to his sisters.

Prayer at Work in the World

"You always hear me."

Think about the times Jesus prayed. On a hillside, in a garden, in front of a tomb. . .never in anything resembling a church.

And yet, all too often we reduce our prayer time to church services on a Sunday.

Imagine there was a tool that could revive and revamp your life—but you were only allowed to use it on a particular day and in a particular way.

There is nothing wrong with praying in church. It is to be encouraged. But don't leave your prayers there.

When Jesus walked the earth, the priests sold the right to have God listen to you. If the proper sacrifice wasn't made, the prayer wouldn't be answered. Jesus dismissed that notion, and the income derived from it, in a very public way.

The world is the church God built. And it isn't only Jesus that God always hears. He hears you in traffic, He hears you at home, He hears you out walking. . .

Of course, prayer is generally a private thing, an intimate conversation, but sometimes, as Jesus proved, others can benefit from hearing prayer at work in the world.

The Answer to Jesus' Prayer

Lazarus came out of the tomb!

We aren't told how he felt about the whole dying thing, but his sisters were overjoyed to have him back. The Pharisees, on hearing about it, were less than delighted and put Lazarus on their "hit list." Imagine deciding to kill a man who had so recently been dead and wasn't anymore! In the end, the Pharisees settled for killing Jesus.

Two things came from this event. Many people, even in a place that had recently rejected Him, came to believe in Jesus Christ because of this resurrection. But not everyone was impressed. Some ran to tell the Pharisees about it. And that was also part of the plan.

This was Jesus' point of no return. This was where He called the Pharisees' bluff.

He had called on God, publicly and directly, for a miracle. And it had been given. If that was possible, then people would begin to wonder why they needed a corrupt and powerful set of priests like the ones currently occupying the temple. After this, the Pharisees really needed to put up or shut up.

They were not going to let Him get away with embarrassing them like that. They had the power to have Him executed. And He was counting on that.

But you have to wonder if no one told them about Jesus saying, "I am the resurrection!"

Practical Prayers

- Almighty God, it is a wonder that You listen to me at all, let alone listen to me all the time. I am sorry for the silly things I say. I can be a bit foolish in the presence of awesome majesty. But I will get better with practice. And I intend to work on that practice!

- My prayers may be private, Lord Jesus, but I hope they are never secret. As You taught those listening outside the tomb, may I also teach friends, family, and strangers that prayer is a powerful thing.

- Dear Lord, may I live my life as a prayer. Understanding that You hear everything, may I talk with You and seek Your advice in every aspect of my life, until it becomes as natural as breathing.

30

"I SWEAR, BY GOD. . .TO DO STUFF HE MIGHT NOT LIKE."

A Prayer Said in Anger

When the king heard the woman's words, he tore his robes.
As he went along the wall, the people looked, and they saw
that, under his robes, he had sackcloth on his body. He said,
"May God deal with me, be it ever so severely, if the head of
Elisha son of Shaphat remains on his shoulders today!"

2 KINGS 6:30–31 NIV

The phrase "May God deal with me ever so severely" is spoken throughout the Old Testament by different people and in different ways. It has been a loving promise, a cry of fear and despair, an emphatic oath, and all too often, a threat.

Ruth promised to face the worst God could do to her if she did not stay by Naomi and help her the best she could, even unto death.

King Saul may have been as upset for himself as for his son when Jonathan unknowingly broke an oath his father had made. Sentencing his son to death, the thought of how severely (he thought) God would punish him was probably uppermost in the king's mind.

Jonathan promised to save David from King Saul's wrath and offered to accept the wrath of the Lord if he failed to do so.

The high priest, Eli, used the threat of the worst the Lord could do to get young Samuel to tell him what he had heard after a heavenly visitation. Samuel wasn't withholding information, but

Eli might have had a bit of a guilty conscience and wanted to cover all the bases.

When King David heard that Abner, a righteous man who had been his enemy and then his ally, had been killed, he grieved and fasted, promising to accept the worst God had to offer if he ate anything before the sun set. Then he promised a kinsman a life-long position in command of his army, accepting God's severest punishment if it proved not to be so.

Queen Jezebel promised to accept the worst her pagan gods could inflict if she didn't kill Elijah within twenty-four hours.

When he heard Adonijah was indulging in some political maneuvering, King Solomon declared that God could do His worst to him if he failed to have his half brother killed.

And, in the verse above, the king of Israel, suffering because of the hardships of his people, cried out in frustration and threatened to execute Elisha for not convincing God to help them in the way he expected Him to.

The Casually Broken Commandment

"OMG!" "Oh, for God's sake!" "God almighty!" Even the name of "Jesus Christ!"

How casually we use these expressions, and others. They have become almost meaningless in everyday conversation, but actually they are exhortations to heaven, to God, to Jesus. We're treating prayer like dirt. And given what we know about the power of prayer, we need to treat it with a bit more respect.

These expressions defy the commandment not to take the Lord's name in vain, and there can't be many commandments broken more regularly that that one. And God doesn't punish us. He probably doesn't even sigh wearily anymore.

As it is so often, the punishment is in the act itself—how it demeans our relationship with God and how foolish it makes us look to be continually saying things we don't mean or don't understand.

"But those expressions are everywhere," you might say.

Sure they are. But they don't have to be in the example you set, and then they won't be in the speech of those who listen to you.

It is possible to reclaim those terms. How do we do that? We stop tossing them around so casually and use them with a little more love. Simple. You just have to do it.

Jesus told us not to swear oaths, to simply be people of our word. Are you up for that? Could you make one of your lifetime missions the abolition of the casual oath and the restoration of the casual (but respectful) prayer?

The Answer to the Prayer for God's Worst

The answers are, of course, as varied as the prayers. God doesn't always seem compelled to take part in prayers that use His name but often aren't really about Him.

The good and virtuous prayers spoken in this way usually need an answer. They are kept. Ruth does care for Naomi all of her days and may well have been buried beside her. Jonathan does warn David when he is in danger and remains a true friend until the end.

Eli, of course, is dealt with severely, in as much as his line is ended in his lifetime and he dies of a broken neck. But that may have had more to do with the behavior of his sons than his promise to Samuel.

Jezebel dies one of the more gruesome deaths in the Bible, so she was very severely dealt with.

Solomon did have Adonijah killed. David did maintain his fast.

King Saul was prevented by his own men from killing his son. Jonathan eventually died alongside his father in battle. You could say Saul was severely dealt with, but uttering thoughtless oaths may have been the least of his problems.

The phrase isn't nearly so common in the New Testament, where Jesus tells us not to swear oaths at all, simply to let our yes be yes and our no be no.

Practical Prayers

- Dear Lord—how often do I begin a prayer with those words without giving any thought to how dear You are and that You are in fact my Lord? If I thought more about those two words, it might lead to fewer situations where I need to pray for help.

- I am not of this world, Lord, You have raised me above it. So remind me from time to time that I do not have to behave and speak as those around me do. May my words and actions reflect the world I am going to rather than the one I live in now.

- May I learn to say nothing, Lord, rather than demean Your name.

31

"WITHOUT YOU, LORD, I AM COMPLETELY VULNERABLE!"

The First Prayer for Mercy

*Cain said to the LORD, "My punishment is more than I can
bear. Today you are driving me from the land, and I will be
hidden from your presence; I will be a restless wanderer
on the earth, and whoever finds me will kill me." But
the LORD said to him, "Not so; anyone who kills Cain will
suffer vengeance seven times over." Then the LORD put a mark
on Cain so that no one who found him would kill him.*

GENESIS 4:13–15 NIV

The very first prayer for mercy was a doozy!

God created Adam and Eve as husband and wife, so you can
imagine He was especially fond of their first two children. Now
imagine how annoyed He would be if someone murdered one of
those children—especially if that someone was the other child!

The first fruit of that very special union was a murderer. God
must have been very tempted to wipe the slate clean and begin
again. Instead, He banished Cain from Eden and promised him a
life of hard labor and wandering.

Cain was understandably (if not justifiably) upset about having to
leave his home, but he seems just as upset about being separated
from God's presence (which God never said would be part of his
punishment). He should have counted himself lucky to get off so
lightly, but it is touching that he feared the loss of God's presence.

Cain seemed to think that without God in his life he would be easy prey for the world. So perhaps he was more worried about his own skin than he was about God turning away from him. Either way, even blinded by anger and hurt feelings he understood that he needed God in his life.

It is interesting to note that Adam and Eve, the parents of both the murderer and his victim, play no part in the resolution of the case. Perhaps they understood more than anyone since then that their lives and the lives of their children were gifts of God and for Him to deal with.

So Cain pleaded his case to the ultimate authority, never once apologizing, but pleading for mercy all the same.

What was a loving, but just, God to do?

I'm Not Sorry I'm Sorry

Oh, the lengths we will go to just so we don't have to take responsibility for our actions!

We will blame our circumstances, our bad luck, our parents, our upbringing, even God Himself. And while we might be able to make a very good case for our actions being someone else's fault, that doesn't help us one bit. It might help us avoid the imminent punishment, but it doesn't help us learn and grow.

And denying our guilt also robs the other person of the opportunity to forgive. Humility and honesty tend to inspire forgiveness and second chances. Refusing to face the truth and passing the buck to someone else just hardens hearts and encourages bitterness.

Cain's prayer was only about his own interest with no thought for his mother, father, or brother. That's why God couldn't leave him in Eden. That attitude would have been a poisonous one.

And it would have been poisonous for Cain as well. Repressed guilt and the fear that causes us to repress it never end well. He shouldn't have been worrying about the hard time the world would give him; he should have been more concerned with the hard time his own unforgiven soul would give him.

Denying our faults doesn't seem to have died out with Cain's descendants. Doing foolish things is in our nature, but learning from his example, we can rise above that trap.

God, our family, and our community just want to know that we understand what we did and that we understand it wasn't anyone's fault but our own. Fess up! And watch the help, love, and forgiveness come in.

The Answer to Cain's Prayer

The one thing God didn't do was forgive Cain and welcome him back into the family. Why not? Well, Cain never asked him to. There was no repentance, and that is an essential part of redemption.

But He did soothe his fears about being killed. The "mark of Cain" was God's way of saying, "This man is mine. If I didn't kill him, you certainly can't." If Cain had chosen to look at it this way, he might also have understood that God was not walking away from him.

The sentence of hard labor and eternal wandering seems to have been ameliorated over time as well. Far from being a nomad, Cain eventually founded a city where he raised his family. He may have been a prosperous man in the area. He named both the city and his son "Enoch," which means "dedication."

If the dedication was to God, then perhaps it meant Cain remembered his love for the Lord and wanted to be reunited with Him.

Going further into the land of speculation, we have to wonder if he ever found the humility to apologize for killing his brother. The fact that his line ended in the flood suggests he didn't.

So, the first plea for mercy received it. But did God ever go so far as to redeem Cain? Well. . .as far as we know, Cain never asked Him to.

Practical Prayers

- Lord, I am sorry! I'm sorry for all the times I wasn't sorry and robbed You of the opportunity to forgive. We both know that's a gift You love to give and I love to receive. So I'm sorry!

- Pride! God our Father, You warned us about pride in ourselves, but still we stand on it like it's a rock that can support us rather than a weight that drags us down. May I spend my life being so proud of You that I never have time to think of myself that way.

- Dear Lord, even when You are perfectly justified in punishing, Your love is still evident. Jonah understood that, and I understand it. I pray that Cain understood it. I pray I always remember it.

32

"I SEE THE SIZE OF THEIR ARMY. LET THEM SEE THE SIZE OF OUR GOD!"

A Prayer for Help against Overwhelming Odds

Zerah the Ethiopian came out against them with an army of a million men and 300 chariots, and came as far as Mareshah. And Asa went out to meet him, and they drew up their lines of battle in the Valley of Zephathah at Mareshah. And Asa cried to the LORD his God, "O LORD, there is none like you to help, between the mighty and the weak. Help us, O LORD our God, for we rely on you, and in your name we have come against this multitude. O LORD, you are our God; let not man prevail against you."

2 CHRONICLES 14:9–11 ESV

Asa was one of the rare good kings in the Bible—mostly!

He followed in the footsteps of his father Abijah, king of Judah. At that time, Judah and Israel were often at war, and Abijah had berated his neighboring brothers for worshipping false idols and refusing to follow the ways of the Lord. Israel had gone so far as to expel the Levites and set up their own priestly caste.

For much of his reign, Asa did what his father had done and what God always wanted His people to do. He did his best to rid the land of Judah of pagan idols and led his people in the ways of the Lord. In return, the Lord gave him peace and prosperity, which he used for the good of the people and to fortify the country's defenses.

It all makes so much sense you have to wonder why all the kings before and after him didn't do it.

Of course, all that prosperity made Judah an attractive prospect for would-be conquerors. So Zerah the Cushite (or Ethiopian) arrayed his army against them. And this was a far bigger, better-equipped army than any Asa could put together.

A king who found his strength in the world might have quickly sought out some allies or come to terms with Zerah. But Asa took his army out to the field of battle. Oh, how the Cushites must have laughed. Looking at the differences in numbers, most of them probably didn't expect to bloody their swords.

Then Asa prayed. And then he attacked!

God and You against the World

"If God is with us, who can stand against us?"

We say it, we sing it, but how much do we really believe it?

Gideon, David, Asa—they all experienced victory against overwhelming odds because they put their trust in God. And those stories were recorded not so we would go recklessly into battle but so we would remember that having God on our side is worth any number of other allies.

Of course, having God on your side really means you being on God's side. And being on God's side will greatly influence the "battles" you fight.

These days, we aren't fighting arrays of armor-clad men and horse-drawn chariots. The battle is much more subtle.

Sure, if it comes to a situation where we are being physically attacked, it is a wonderful thing to be able to call on the Lord, but most of our battles will be societal ones, relationship ones.

Our greatest victories will lie in convincing someone there is more to life; in avoiding the traps of this world and showing others how to do the same; in spreading the gospel and sharing the love of God; in opening eyes to the works of the world and its "prince" and showing them there is a way out.

"Just me against the world?" you might ask. At times it might seem like that, but it's far from the case. Millions of believers are engaged in the same battle. But even if it was just you against the world it still wouldn't be *just* you, it would be you and God. And those are very good odds!

The Answer to Asa's Prayer

They won!

With God on their side, they beat the Cushite army so badly it seemed like it might never recover. Then the men of Judah got a bit carried away and went on a victorious rampage. They probably thought they made up for it by dedicating their spoils of gold and silver to God.

What a stunning example of faith in the Lord!

You would think He would have remembered it.

Sadly, men are not the most consistent of creatures.

In getting rid of pagan practices, Asa even cut down his grand-mother's Asherah pole. That shows a certain amount of determination. But he left the "high places," where pagan sacrifices were still made. So it was a good attempt, but he didn't finish the job.

Sometime afterward, another massive army marched on Judah. So, of course you would think Asa would pray and ride to victory once again, wouldn't you?

No. This time, older and perhaps wearier, he took the gold and silver that was dedicated to God after the last battle and bought himself an ally.

They won the war, but a prophet reminded him of his lack of faith and predicted the country would forever be at war after that. Asa responded by jailing the prophet.

Even when he succumbed to an illness in later life, Asa refused to call on God for help.

Pride won that battle. And Asa lost!

Practical Prayers

- Lord, it's all in the approach. If I am not wholeheartedly for You, then the enemy will find a way to undo the work. May I be completely *in* You so I, and my work, will be completely protected *by* You.

- Almighty God, there is no battle You cannot win, but there are battles You wouldn't fight. Pride might blind me to the difference, so may love open my eyes to the distinction.

- May I always remember, Lord, that victories gained through You are Your victories, lest I get a little too full of myself and think I'm doing the work.

33

"SHE'S MY SISTER, LORD, NOT MY ENEMY!"

A Prayer That God Would Heal One He Had Cursed

When the cloud lifted from above the tent, Miriam's skin was leprous—it became as white as snow. Aaron turned toward her and saw that she had a defiling skin disease, and he said to Moses, "Please, my lord, I ask you not to hold against us the sin we have so foolishly committed. Do not let her be like a stillborn infant coming from its mother's womb with its flesh half eaten away." So Moses cried out to the LORD, "Please, God, heal her!"

NUMBERS 12:10–13 NIV

Miriam and Aaron were only part of the Exodus story because of their brother, Moses. The book of Numbers tells us that Moses was one of the humblest men in the world, but his siblings were jealous of the attention he was getting from God.

So they complained. Doubtless they convinced each other they were perfectly justified—but they complained. Behind his back. And they used Moses' Cushite wife as an excuse to criticize their brother.

But, really, they wanted to know why God didn't talk to them as much as He did to Moses. After all, Miriam had saved Moses' life when he was a baby by placing him in the way of the Egyptian princess, and Moses had only agreed to lead his people to freedom on the assurance that Aaron would help him.

We don't know who came up with the complaint or who made the most/worst of it, but we do know who bore the brunt of the punishment.

God came down in a column of smoke and called both of them out. He explained that Moses was more than just a prophet—he was a particular favorite of the Almighty, and who were they to criticize that arrangement?

At that moment, they must surely have been regretting their wish for God to pay more attention to them. Before they could protest their innocence, "the anger of the Lord burned against them" (Numbers 12:9 NIV).

It must have been something like standing too close to a nuclear reaction. When the Lord disappeared, Miriam was left with a disfigured face. Aaron seems to have been left unblemished, but he pleaded with Moses that their sister should not be punished for the crime they both committed.

Moses seems to have been every bit as stunned as Aaron. He heard his brother's plea and called out to the Lord.

Time-Out before You Act Out

Have you ever had a week of purification? (We're not talking detox or juicing here.) Well, have you ever had time to cool down and understand you were making a big fuss over next to nothing?

Same thing!

We can hope and be reassured that Miriam's skin was restored over the week she spent outside the camp in her own tent, but for the whole thing to be worthwhile, her heart would have to be restored too.

She was a powerful, influential woman among her people, but for a while she had acted like a child and threatened the safety of her people. If she (and Aaron) had elbowed their way into an area that rightly belonged to Moses, his leadership would have been jeopardized. Where they had one man listening to God and leading the people, they would have had the potential for three-way squabbles and confusion.

God had chosen Moses for a very special task, which would bring him no great benefit in earthly terms. The best thing anyone else could do was understand this and support it. Hopefully Miriam came to the same conclusion as she waited and thought in her tent.

Personal ambition is a very easy trap to fall into. And once it gets a grip on us, we will do ridiculous things to support it. We can often lose sight of the greater good. That's where some purification can be useful.

If you find yourself undermining anyone, or convinced you can do a better job, or feeling unfairly treated, take some time (hopefully before you get put out of the camp) to examine your motives, to put your case to God and listen to His reply, to purify your heart before the damage is done.

The Answer to Moses' Prayer

In describing his sister's face, Aaron makes reference to flesh peeling off. The disfigurement must have appeared shocking in the extreme.

God, however, is not cruel. The punishment had a purpose. The Israelites needed a single leader, and anyone undermining that leader's authority diluted the authority of the Lord. He also responded to Moses' prayer.

Miriam would have been an elderly lady at this point and a respected prophetess in her own right, but God compared His punishment to a father chastising a child, which suggests it has a limited time span.

We are not actually told that Miriam was healed in response to her brother's prayer, and we hear very little of her after this situation. God said she should be placed outside the Israelites' camp for a week of purification. The love of her brother and the esteem she was held in by the people meant that the entire nation (nomads at that time) waited for her purification period to be completed before moving on.

There would have been no point to that week and no purpose in the delay if Miriam's purification hadn't also involved healing.

Practical Prayers

- Leadership is really no joyride. If I am called to it, Lord, keep me humble. If not, keep me supportive.

- If what was in our hearts showed up on our faces, Lord, You know we would all be expelled from the camp. Purify my heart in such a way that I would not mind if everyone saw it—as You do.

- Bitterness and resentment. Almighty God, if I am feeling those emotions then I should know I am not on Your path. Those are the destructive works of the devil. If I don't walk away from them willingly, then I pray You remove them from me in whatever way You see fit. But I pray I have the strength to walk away willingly.

34

"JESUS, MAY I FOLLOW IN YOUR—WATERY—FOOTSTEPS?"

A Prayer to Transcend "Reality"

But the boat by this time was a long way from the land, beaten by the waves, for the wind was against them. And in the fourth watch of the night he came to them, walking on the sea. But when the disciples saw him walking on the sea, they were terrified, and said, "It is a ghost!" and they cried out in fear. But immediately Jesus spoke to them, saying, "Take heart; it is I. Do not be afraid." And Peter answered him, "Lord, if it is you, command me to come to you on the water."

MATTHEW 14:24–28 ESV

Jesus was at that point in His career where He couldn't go anywhere without attracting a crowd. Not even to grieve for His friend John the Baptist. The disciples knew that and followed after Him. Maybe they thought they could persuade the people to have some sensitivity and come back another day, but instead they ended up helping Him feed five thousand "fans."

When it was all over, Jesus still hadn't had much in the way of time alone, so He told the disciples to take the boat and head back home without Him. Perhaps they thought they would come back for Him in the morning.

But it was a wild night. The boat was tacking into the wind, and it was taking them all night to get anywhere. They may have been taking turns to catch some shut-eye.

Peter must have wondered if he was still asleep when, around the breaking of dawn, he looked over the stern of the boat and saw Jesus walking toward them. Here was a miracle they hadn't seen before. The Lord was walking on water—and making better time than they were in the boat!

You might think that by this time the disciples would have been beyond surprising, but they were fairly shocked by this occurrence. Some of them thought that Jesus must have died and this was His ghost haunting them.

The strangeness of the situation would explain Peter asking, "Is it You?" But not even his normally impetuous nature could explain what happened next. Only faith makes any sense of it.

"Take me out there with You," he said (or words to that effect). Then, and not for the last time, Peter stepped off a boat in pursuit of Jesus.

Stepping Out of the Boat

Jesus could have said, "Sit down, Peter, you're not Me!"

But He didn't. He uttered one word in response to Peter's seemingly foolish idea. He simply said, "Come!"

Few of the miracles Jesus performed were His sole domain, and He never berated anyone for trying. The disciples would go on to heal people, Peter would raise the dead, countless miracles have been performed in His name since then, and for a few steps at least, Peter walked on water.

When Jesus asked people to follow Him, He seems to have meant in every way. (With the possible exception of personal resurrection because He prepared a better option.)

When we commit to following Jesus, we generally commit to getting out of the boat—or leaving our comfort zone. Following

Him, you will find yourself in surprising situations and doing amazing things. Perhaps the biggest surprise will be finding yourself capable of these amazing things. New life in Jesus shows itself in many ways.

The changes can be quite startling. If only there was a book or something we could read that would prepare us. Oh, there is! The Bible. And the transformation of Peter from a hot-headed, rough-and-ready fisherman to a miracle-working statesman is a fine example of the difference Jesus can make in a life.

So ask Him if you can join Him on the biggest adventure of your life. And He will say, "Come!" Then leave the boat—and keep believing as you walk.

The Answer to Peter's Prayer

Peter, the fisherman who had spent most of his days relying on boats to keep him afloat, walked on water.

For that moment, when he absolutely trusted in the power of Jesus, it must have seemed to Peter like anything was possible. What could he not do through Jesus Christ who enabled him to walk on water?

It must have been a euphoric moment. But the thing about those moments is they disappear as quickly as they arrive. Peter "saw the wind" (Matthew 12:30 ESV) and the earthly reality hit home. He was walking on water and that wasn't possible!

As soon as he focused on what he knew could and couldn't happen and not on Jesus, he started to sink. Now Peter could swim, but he was fully dressed and the sea was stormy. He was, very quickly, in real trouble.

So he focused again on Jesus and called out for help. Jesus grabbed him, berated him for his lack of faith, and then they both got into the boat. Whether they both walked to the boat or Jesus dragged a spluttering Peter all the way we aren't told.

One thing we are told is that once they got into the boat the wind died down.

Could it be that He who controls the sky and sea had been testing Peter's faith with a few extra gusts?

Practical Prayers

- Sweet Jesus, the most amazing thing about Peter's story for me is not the steps he took on the water or the fact that You saved him from sinking. It's that he got out of the boat in the first place. Give me the courage to take that first step and turn the rest over to You.

- For every wonderful thing You do in my life, Lord, there will be distractions. That's no coincidence. They will be tests or enemy actions. By focusing always on You, Lord Jesus, I intend to ignore the latter and pass the former.

- Wondrous things, Lord! Time and again the disciples saw Your wonders and doubted or were afraid. The other way to respond would be amazement and delight. In a world that is full of Your wonders, may I always choose the second option.

35

"HERE'S WHAT OTHERS DO, MY SON, AND HERE'S WHAT GOD WANTS YOU TO DO!"

A Prayer for the Fullness of Christian Life

For the love of money is a root of all kinds of evil. Some people, eager for money, have wandered from the faith and pierced themselves with many griefs. But you, man of God, flee from all this, and pursue righteousness, godliness, faith, love, endurance and gentleness. Fight the good fight of the faith. Take hold of the eternal life to which you were called when you made your good confession in the presence of many witnesses.

1 TIMOTHY 6:10–12 NIV

The letters to Timothy are words of instruction to a young follower, but Paul was talking both *about* God *to* Timothy and *to* God *about* Timothy.

The fact that this particular section ends with the word *Amen* raises it to the level of a prayer. But as is so often the case in Paul's epistles (and should be the case with us more often), it can sometimes be difficult to tell ordinary speech from reverent prayer.

Timothy, a man of two worlds with a Jewish mother and a Gentile father, became a follower of Paul while the latter was on his travels, and Paul trusted him with the mission of staying in Ephesus to keep the church there "on message."

Paul's letters to Timothy are full of instructions and advice. At this particular time, it seems that many had forgotten the basics of the faith. Even in those early days, people often thought some esoteric knowledge was necessary for true salvation, and money had a corrupting effect in the church.

Paul has much higher hopes for Timothy though, and prophecies were made that back up these expectations. He gave Timothy hints and instructions. Then he turned, with genuine concern, to Timothy himself. He advised him to take a little wine for his health's sake. Like almost everyone in the Bible, Timothy was a human being with human frailties and had many illnesses.

Then Paul got to the heart of the personal aspect of his letter. "But, you, man of God. . ." he wrote. And there is so much in those few simple words. If you are a man of God or a woman of God then what awesome things might be expected of you?

Paul laid it on the line. The awesome, powerful, world-shaking things God expects of you are. . .faith, love, endurance, and that you seek godliness and justice, that you fight the good fight of faith.

How do those "soft" attributes stack up against the powers of the world? Well, they've done pretty well for more than two thousand years now.

You! In the Middle of It All

Paul listed false doctrine, love of money, gossip, suspicion, division. He went on to talk about righteousness, faith, love, endurance, godliness, fighting the good fight of faith.

Do you know what is between those two lists? Okay, there is a chapter heading, "Paul's Charge to Timothy," but if we take that out of the way, what lies between those two lists is "You, man of God."

In these modern times, just as in ancient times, those two lists are still battling it out, still exerting a pull on our hearts and our attentions. Paul tells us in no uncertain terms to "flee" from the first group and "pursue" the second group.

There isn't really a middle ground. In this battle, not committing is actually the same as committing—to the losing side. Faith and common sense tell us we need to run from one side toward the other. That doesn't mean we won't get entangled in some negative stuff from time to time, but the further into the good we run the more protected from the bad we are.

This coincides nicely with another of Paul's analogies, that of running a good race.

So we need to be moving. And we need to be moving in the right direction.

But it's a long race and there are many distractions. What we need is a constant reminder of what we are running from and what we are running toward. That might be godly company, Bible readings, or a little voice in the back of your head saying, "And as for you, child of God. How are you doing?"

The Answer to Paul's Prayer

We don't know a lot about Timothy, but references made to him elsewhere in Acts and the other Epistles indicate a godly man that Paul was justified in trusting. Church tradition has it that he died a bishop and a martyr to the faith.

In the second letter to his protégé, Paul described how Timothy kept learning because he knew the people who were teaching him. Unnumbered souls across countless generations have learned from these words of instruction, not because they knew Paul personally but because they were intimately acquainted with the one who taught Paul—Jesus Christ!

The apostle Paul had a talent for avoiding complicated theological diversions and keeping the basic good news of the gospel. He brings so much of that neatly to mind when he says (something like), "Okay, man or woman of God. Here's all that is asked of you. How are you doing with that?"

That gentle reminder, and our response, means that Paul's prayer for Timothy goes on being answered today, in each of us.

Practical Prayers

- The distractions are obvious, Lord, but no less effective for that. May I find my own version of Paul to encourage me in my travels.

- The things Paul encourages Timothy toward are all good, life-affirming attributes. Why, Father God, do I struggle with pursuing them? Perhaps it is in someone else's interest that I fail. Shield me from that adversary, Lord, so I might run all the faster to You.

- Flee from? Or run toward? Both are good advice. But, Lord, I would pray that my attention be so focused on You that there is no space for the negative, only for the positive, and that my race for home might be a wholly joyful one.

36

"LORD, THEY ARE KILLING ME! DON'T HOLD IT AGAINST THEM."

A Prayer in Imitation of Christ

Then they cast him out of the city and stoned him. And the witnesses laid down their garments at the feet of a young man named Saul. And as they were stoning Stephen, he called out, "Lord Jesus, receive my spirit." And falling to his knees he cried out with a loud voice, "Lord, do not hold this sin against them." And when he had said this, he fell asleep.

ACTS 7:58–60 ESV

It was the epic battle between the Grecian-Jewish converts and the Hebraic-Jewish converts.

Perhaps you heard of it? Or perhaps not. It was a little matter of fairness in charitable giving, but it assumed a major importance among the people on both sides. So much so that it was hampering "the ministry of the Word" (Acts 6:4 ESV).

Seven men were chosen to heal the rift, and first among them was Stephen, "a man full of faith and of the Holy Spirit" (Acts 6:5 ESV). He was trusted on both sides, perhaps because like the angel that confronted Joshua, the only side he took was God's.

The healing that came about—even though it was political rather than physical—increased the number of believers, which brought Stephen to the attention of some devout Jews. They didn't like what he was preaching and had him arrested on charges of denying the temple and the Mosaic Law.

When he was called to answer these charges, Stephen appeared to have the face of an angel. Perhaps he was secretly delighted that their own court would force them to listen to what he was about to say. He then recounted the history of the Jewish people, reminding the listeners how often God had objected to the idea of being housed in one building and pointing out how they had consistently abused their own prophets.

It was a long, courageous speech, leading up to an accusation of the murder of Jesus Christ.

In the time-honored tradition of human beings (who don't have God in their hearts), they did not take this well. They dragged Stephen out of the city and stoned him.

Knowing he was not going to survive the experience, Stephen showed the depth of his devotion to Jesus and responded even as his Lord did at the end—he asked God to forgive the people who were killing him.

The Surprising Power of Soft Stuff

Forgiveness is like love in several ways. For those who don't really practice either of them, the single most obvious connection is that they are both soft options, ways to get taken advantage of.

Even those of us who claim to practice Christian values often have a difficult time with forgiveness. We imagine others will think us fools, easy to take advantage of, laughable. . .and we let our fear of what the world (or our neighbors, or our colleagues) might think get in the way of emulating our Lord's dying prayer.

Overcoming that fear is part of what makes forgiveness anything but soft or easy or foolish. The people for whom it seems to come naturally, who seem to do it so effortlessly, also have to overcome that fear, but perhaps they have done it often enough to see the effects it has.

Being forgiven, to a heart that sees the world as a place where you have to hurt because you will be hurt, can be a real shock. It might not stop that person from throwing the stone, but it will be startling enough to live in their hearts a while. And that's when strange things happen.

We aren't called on to change people. We are called on to change ourselves and let others see the change. Forgiving people who wrong us—like God has done continually—is perhaps the most powerful way to show our faith. We put the notion, the possibility, of another way into the hearts of people we meet. We plant the seed. And God waters it.

It goes against every instinct. That's what makes it so shockingly powerful!

The Answer to Stephen's Prayer

The immediate answer to Stephen's prayer would not be an obvious one. Whether God held the stone throwers' actions against them or not, we won't know this side of heaven.

Things immediately went from bad to worse. Fired up by this event, the Jews began a great persecution. The disciples were scattered. Many were imprisoned. How could any good come of a situation like that?

Well, the Christian church has always spoken most strongly to the dispossessed. Here, the church itself became like the dispossessed. Those who were jailed would have met others in jail who needed to hear the gospel. The disciples, we are told, performed miracles in lands they might not have visited if they hadn't been chased out of town.

And Paul stepped up his mission to wipe the Christians out.

We aren't told that he participated in the killing—but his approval of it was significant enough to be noted. There and then it seems to have spurred him on to more hatred. How it played on his conscience after he met Stephen's Lord we can only imagine, but it probably helped shape the great man he became.

In that at least, Stephen's prayer was answered directly. The man who seemed to have given approval to his killing was certainly forgiven.

Practical Prayers

- Forgiveness, Lord. It makes no sense. Thankfully I don't have to understand how it does what it does. I just have to know it is one of Your most powerful tools!

- Father God, I have my reasons. I can justify not forgiving. Intellectually, I know it would be a bad move. But I also know You could level all the same reasons at me—yet You chose not to and You forgive. Help me willingly give what I willingly receive.

- Dear Lord, sweet Jesus, how can I claim to be a follower of Yours and not do what You do? Forgive me!

37

"LORD, IT WASN'T EASY, BUT WE SPOKE ABOUT YOU AND SAW RESULTS."

A Prayer for the Courage to Speak Your Faith

"And now, Lord, look upon their threats and grant to your servants to continue to speak your word with all boldness, while you stretch out your hand to heal, and signs and wonders are performed through the name of your holy servant Jesus." And when they had prayed, the place in which they were gathered together was shaken, and they were all filled with the Holy Spirit and continued to speak the word of God with boldness.

ACTS 4:29–31 ESV

Imagine it in slow motion, movie style! It's the point where the underdog has had enough and sets out to confront his or her nemesis.

The Holy Spirit had descended on a scared bunch of ordinary guys, turning them into the apostles who, in Jesus' name, would change the world. They banded together, prayed, encouraged each other—then stepped out into the world.

Entering the temple at prayer time, Peter and John met a crippled beggar at the Beautiful Gate. Peter told the man he had no silver or gold to give, but he could give healing in the name of Jesus Christ. And the man was healed.

Peter and John were instant sensations and the crowds gathered round them, so they shared the gospel.

The temple at that time was a big operation and had to be kept running smoothly, not least because the priests depended on it for their income. Anything interrupting the smooth flow of worshippers and the steady *clink-clink* of offerings was bound to attract attention.

The temple guards arrested them and locked them up overnight.

Full of their own authority, they asked the apostles by what power they had healed the crippled beggar. They thought it was sorcery.

Completely vulnerable, and unused to speaking to people in authority, Peter found himself undaunted. The Holy Spirit filled him. He told them that Jesus Christ had healed the man, yes, even the same Jesus Christ they had put to death on the cross.

The priests were stumped. The lame man whom they all knew was standing there, healed, and they had no other explanation. But more than that, they knew the apostles to be ordinary, uneducated men and could not understand the authority they spoke with.

After some confusion, bluster, and threats on the part of the priest, Peter and John were set free. In awe themselves over what had happened, they reported back to the rest of the believers. The other believers prayed that, given the obvious power in the words of the Lord, they too would have the courage to proclaim them.

Fear, Pray, Speak, Wow!

In a world already antagonistic to the Christian faith, we sometimes make things easier for it.

The worldly powers have always been against the Christian faith. It's not some new persecution, and it shouldn't really surprise anyone. The Christian faith, fully implemented, would turn the world upside down.

But sometimes we collude with that antipathy in keeping quiet about our beliefs. It's all very well to say, "It's a personal thing," and it is, but it was never meant to be only a personal thing. It's all very well to say, "I'll let someone else do the preaching," but the people you meet aren't anyone else's responsibility.

Let's face it, we keep it to ourselves because we are afraid of how talking about it might make us look.

The frustrating thing about that is that if everyone who was nervous about looking weird because they talked about their faith actually talked about their faith, it would soon be the nonbelievers who would be the odd ones out.

The disciples knew what that fear felt like. They prayed, they tried, they saw amazing results, and they just kept on going.

Most of those being stopped by fear these days won't have gone as far as praying sincerely about it. And they will miss out on the wonderful results.

And, hey, if we all prayed before we spoke. . .wouldn't that make the world a better place all by itself?

The Answer to the Believers' Prayer

The earth moved.

Perhaps the last time they felt something like that was when Jesus died, so they must have been certain their prayer had been heard.

And it came true. They did proclaim the gospel, way more than was good for them (in earthly terms). They went out on their separate missions (or stayed in Jerusalem), they taught about the Lord to anyone who would listen, and they almost always came up against earthly powers who told them to shut up. And they kept teaching, all but one of them dying violently because they no longer feared to proclaim Jesus.

It is an abiding problem for those who would say Jesus was anything other than God in human form. They cannot deny the disciples were ordinary people with not much in the way of education, resources, or any tradition of authority between them. They are sometimes portrayed as foolish, even cowardly, and they ran and hid at their leader's moment of greatest need.

But it also can't be denied that something happened after that, and they became a force to be reckoned with. Something happened that each of them was willing to sacrifice their life for or be tortured for.

Pick a dozen working guys at random and ask what it would take to get them to do the same.

Practical Prayers

- Beloved Jesus, You didn't come only for me. You played Your part. May I have the courage, at least, to tell others about it.

- In Your parable of the ninety-nine and the one, Jesus, You told of the shepherd braving the rocks and the storms to bring home that one lost lamb. Rock and storm I don't have to face, I simply have to tell the next lost lamb I meet that You are looking for them.

- Almighty God, if You are with me, why should I fear any other power? And if I am not afraid, I should tell people why I am not afraid, so they might be set free from fear as well.

38

"EVEN IN ADVERSITY, GOD, PEOPLE ARE LISTENING. SO WE'LL SING OF YOU."

A Prayer in Chains

About midnight Paul and Silas were praying and singing hymns to God, and the other prisoners were listening to them. Suddenly there was such a violent earthquake that the foundations of the prison were shaken. At once all the prison doors flew open, and everyone's chains came loose. The jailer woke up, and when he saw the prison doors open, he drew his sword and was about to kill himself because he thought the prisoners had escaped.

ACTS 16:25–27 NIV

It is amazing how preaching love and life can get you into trouble!

Paul had previously been stoned and thrown out of cities for it. Now, in Philippi, he and Silas were jailed for something similar. But it wasn't his preaching that caused the trouble this time. They were locked up for disrupting business as usual.

He and Silas were spreading the Word, but a slave girl kept following them, shouting that they were men of God who knew the secret of salvation. You would think that was good free advertising, but it troubled Paul. This girl could predict the future, and her owners made a lot of money out of that strange ability. Paul believed that this ability was the result of a demonic possession. Isn't it strange how often demons declare Jesus and His followers in the Bible?

Finally, Paul, in the name of Jesus, told the demon to leave her, and with it went her predictive powers. Nobody seems to have seen that coming!

Her owners were incensed! Their money-making seer was now no more than an ordinary girl to them. They dragged Paul and Silas through the city to the elders and made some random accusations of disruption and strange practices against them. These men must have had considerable influence because they managed to get the crowd and the elders on their side. Paul and Silas were stripped and flogged severely before being thrown in jail.

Most people would have spent the night writhing in pain (prison beds in those days not being famously comfortable). Paul and Silas, however, understanding that people in jail probably needed the gospel more than most, spent the night singing praises and praying.

The other prisoners may have been impressed by their fortitude—but they may also have thought they were nuts. Until they saw and felt the results of those prayers!

God Will Take You There, and Out Again

Try it. Preach the Word in the ordinary places of life. It will probably get you into trouble. And that's something most of us try to avoid.

Paul knew all about the trouble inflicted on Christians. He used to inflict it! But still he kept walking into it, time and again. Why? Well, partly because he really had no choice. He had a message inside him that couldn't be contained. And partly because the Word is of most use in places of trouble.

The people in the market place needed to hear the gospel, but the people in the jail, whether guilty of their crimes or victims of the system, had a greater need.

For Paul, who had already been diverted in his travels by the Holy Spirit, being "diverted" into jail was just another way of going where he was sent. God put him there, God would get him out. Knowing that was probably what kept him singing.

And those of us who don't find ourselves persecuted for our faith might also learn from the example and deliberately take the Word to places of trouble—places of need.

Jesus had already told the other disciples of the importance of visiting the prisoner, feeding the hungry, and so on. Here were Paul and Silas "visiting" the prisoners.

If that's not your thing, then there are always the hungry, the homeless, the lonely, the grieving. . .

The Answer to Paul and Silas's Prayer

We aren't told what Paul and Silas prayed for, but that doesn't mean we can't understand the answer.

In this man-made prison, in the presence of others trapped by the same earthly system, Paul and Silas prayed. The others listened. Some may have joined in. And all were set free.

There was an earthquake so violent it shook the foundations of the prison. We don't hear of anything being destroyed, but, in a heavenly display of precision bombing, all the cell doors popped open and all the shackles fell off the prisoners.

The prison guard who had been charged with taking special care of Paul and Silas was about to kill himself, convinced all his charges would have run for freedom. But Paul, showing concern for his jailer, says, "Don't harm yourself. We are all still here."

What he understood was that even in chains they were free men in Christ. And that God has the ability to set us free from any of the cages this world will try to put us in. The same is still true today.

The jailer, perhaps sensing that the God of these men already cared more for him than his earthly masters, became a convert on the spot and took Paul and Silas home to care for their wounds.

Like the slave girl and the other prisoners (of whom we hear no more), he may well have gone on to become a member of the Christian church in Philippi. It would be difficult to imagine the experience leaving their hearts unchanged.

Practical Prayers

- Almighty God, if I believe in You, then I have to believe You guide my steps—even when I don't like where they take me. Remind me to look beyond the obvious, to find the need, and to put Your love where it may not have been before.

- Dear Lord, chains and iron gates make a very effective image of a jail. But people walk through this life carrying their emotional prisons with them. Help me to help You to help them be free.

- Sweet Jesus, the freedom found in You can be found in a prison cell, in the grip of illness, even on a cross. I will never forget, whatever my circumstance, that You died to set me free. Now all I need to do is share this freedom, whatever the circumstance.

39

"THIS IS HOW YOU SPEAK TO THE ALMIGHTY."

Prayer as Taught by Jesus

"This, then, is how you should pray: 'Our Father in heaven, hallowed be your name, your kingdom come, your will be done, on earth as it is in heaven. Give us today our daily bread. And forgive us our debts, as we also have forgiven our debtors. And lead us not into temptation, but deliver us from the evil one.' For if you forgive other people when they sin against you, your heavenly Father will also forgive you. But if you do not forgive others their sins, your Father will not forgive your sins."

MATTHEW 6:9–15 NIV

Jesus had just laid out His manifesto.

He talked about the blessed (who are apparently not the people his listeners expected). He talked about being salt and light, about the law, about murder, adultery, divorce, swearing oaths, seeking revenge (and how destructive it is), loving your enemies (shockingly), giving to the needy—and then He got to prayer.

But first He told his audience how not to pray. The practice of prayer must have fallen into a sad state of disrepair if God's chosen people needed a lesson on how not to pray.

They were told prayer isn't a performance to be put on for the benefit of others, and it shouldn't be always asking for things because God knows your needs. And God doesn't need to have it all explained to Him at great length.

Simple, short, and appreciative seem to be the way to go.

Then He taught His listeners what became known as the Lord's Prayer.

"Our Father in heaven, hallowed be your name" acknowledges God as our heavenly Father and glorifies His name.

"Your kingdom come, your will be done, on earth as it is in heaven" places proper emphasis on the will of God in our lives.

"Give us today our daily bread" is the only material request made, and it may well be simply acknowledging that God does, indeed, supply our needs.

"Forgive us our debts, as we also have forgiven our debtors, and lead us not into temptation, but deliver us from the evil one" refer to heavenly matters such as forgiveness and the eternal battle between good and evil. In early versions, the prayer ends here. And Jesus went back to reiterate the line about forgiveness, suggesting that it is only in forgiving others that forgiveness for ourselves might truly be found.

Forgiveness is of such importance that Jesus includes it in His example of perfect prayer—and returned to it immediately afterward.

It is the one thing that our prayer to God, as taught by His Son, requires of us.

Now, isn't that a challenging thought?

Old-Fashioned, Yet Up-to-Date

People are always on the lookout for something new. There is no shortage of spiritual leaders willing to tell us a new way to commune with God, the universe, or whatever. Some are attractive, some are interesting, but the fashions come and the fashions go.

Sometimes we almost dismiss the old ways like the Lord's Prayer just because our parents did it and our grandparents did it (so it *must* be old-fashioned). We want something that applies to our lives. But the Lord's Prayer would have been old-fashioned in our great-grandparents' day too. They said it because it was perfect for their generation, as did the generation before, and the generation before. Things that don't apply equally to each new generation don't tend to stick around too long.

Now imagine you had a way you preferred people to get in touch with you. If they do it this way they stand a better chance of getting your attention—and a response. It works for you and because of that, it is better for the ones trying to reach you. And you tell them this.

And then you discover they have been asking their neighbor the best way to get in touch with you, or the local football coach, or the cashier. But you already told them.

God, in the person of Jesus, already told us the best way to get in touch with Him. Why would we listen to anyone else?

The Answer to Jesus' Prayer

Immediately after teaching His audience how to pray properly, Jesus carried on with His "manifesto," covering issues like fasting, worrying, judging, etc. But He Himself returned to the repeated theme of forgiveness in His ministry, even as He died on the cross. "Father, forgive them. . ."

There is no possible way to quantify the answers to the Lord's Prayer. Even trying to imagine the number of times it has been prayed would cause the greatest intellect to stagger. It has been said in school classes by rows of children, in churches by halls of worshippers, at bedtimes by individual believers, hurriedly by people in desperate circumstances, by people who have said it so often they don't stop to think about it, all across the world and by as many generations as can be fit into twenty centuries.

Surely God knows the answers to all of those prayers, but it would require more than all the trees in the world to make the books to list them.

As for the rest of us, we need to keep praying the Lord's Prayer and experiencing those answers for ourselves.

Practical Prayers

- Kneeling down to pray, hands clasped, eyes closed, seems so old-fashioned, so childish. But if I kneel, my sins kneel also. And if I become as a child, then, Father God, isn't that a good thing?

- Dear Lord, Your prayer has stood the test of the centuries. It can surely last my lifetime. I just need to keep applying its eternal truths to my changing situations.

- The simplest of truths are sometimes the most difficult to see, so for the gift of Your prayer, dear Lord, and the clarity it brings to my life, I thank You.

40

"ALMIGHTY GOD, LOOK HOW COOL I AM."

A Prayer with No Humility

*To some who were confident of their own righteousness
and looked down on everyone else, Jesus told this parable:
"Two men went up to the temple to pray, one a Pharisee
and the other a tax collector. The Pharisee stood by himself
and prayed: 'God, I thank you that I am not like other
people—robbers, evildoers, adulterers—or even like this tax
collector. I fast twice a week and give a tenth of all I get.'"*

LUKE 18:9–12 NIV

This was a parable, but if you're wondering whether the Lord had anyone in mind when He told it, you only have to ask if you've met anyone like this Pharisee.

The answer will likely be yes. Most of us have met blowhards like that, and they usually give their religion a bad reputation.

The man was a Pharisee, so he would have been educated in the Law of Moses and would have benefited financially from encouraging others to follow it. He knew what he was supposed to be and had spent most of his life practicing the rituals that would supposedly make him that "godly" man.

What he didn't understand was that he had made an idol of his religion, and of himself. . .and completely missed the point and purpose of his faith.

The Pharisee stood apart from the others at the temple and prayed. In some translations, it says he prayed about himself. He gave thanks that he kept the commandments and wasn't like all the other people. You know, all the others that God must surely despise just like he did. He fasted, he tithed—and he thought this somehow made him better than the other worshippers who stood around him.

He may even have done his praying/boasting out loud, which must really have charmed the others.

By the standards of the society he lived in, the Pharisee was a successful and righteous man. A man of influence. A role model. Above reproach. Jesus was about to use him to redefine what God saw as worthy—and not in a way the Pharisee or any of his admirers would appreciate.

Everyone Else Has a Problem. I'm Just Fine

In all likelihood, this Pharisee would have been born into his position. Is that what made him so special? He would have been educated in a way the masses weren't. Is that what made him better than them? And he would have lived off the offerings they gave from their hard-earned income. Is that what gave him the right to look down on them?

None of what he thought made him special was really his doing. And the same is true today with people who think themselves better than others. Their conceit, their lack of humility, is just as much a problem in the eyes of God as whatever habit or behavioral pattern the "lesser" people indulge in.

The attitude isn't the problem. The problem is the lack of awareness of the problem. God judged that Pharisee even as the man was telling God how awesome he was. Sure, his fasting and tithing were all well and good, but his humility and his kindness to others needed more than a little work.

With the awareness of our faults, we can do something about them; we can improve, and that's what Jesus wants for us. The cry of "Forgive me, I am a sinner" isn't so we feel dreadful about ourselves, it is so we can accept our sins and get to work, with God's help, on overcoming them.

The moment we think we are perfect, we have an obvious problem.

No one would like to think of Jesus watching them as He watched the Pharisee. So we tell ourselves we aren't that bad. And it's probably true.

But imagine looking at yourself through the Lord's eyes. Give yourself some love as He does, but look honestly and ask, "Lord, what would You have me work on here?"

The Answer to the Pharisee's Prayer

Jesus compared the Pharisee to a man who was an obvious sinner and despised in his community, but that man knows his faults and begs forgiveness for them. This man, a tax collector, Jesus tells His audience, was the one God looked most favorably upon.

Imagine what a shock that would have been to the proud Pharisee. In fact, imagine what a shock that would have been to most people back then, including the tax collector!

Stories like this were part of the reason the Pharisees hated Jesus so much. People listened to Him, and the stories He told had the power to destroy their version of society. Jesus threatened their livelihood, their power, and their pride. People have killed and been killed for less.

The answer to the prayer of the man who inspired this parable was, in all likelihood, a humbling experience. Hopefully, it did him good.

Ironically, the term *Pharisee* means "set apart," as in one set apart for service to God. In setting himself physically and spiritually apart from other worshippers, this particular Pharisee became the example of what was wrong with the priestly caste at the time. Whereas He, Jesus, lived, walked, and died with the common people.

Practical Prayers

- It might be difficult, Lord, to see myself from the outside. So let me begin by sincerely asking You to show me how You see me.

- Almighty God, one way or another, all I have came from You. What do I have to be proud about or to boast about? Nothing except You and Your completely undeserved love for me.

- We humans like guidelines and absolutes, dear Jesus. It's what makes the Law so attractive. It's something to stand on and beat our chests about. But You fulfilled the Law by bringing it to life in love. And love, as we know, is a variable, ever-growing thing. Give me the confidence to let go of my pride and lose myself in Your love.

41

"YOU? AM I PERSECUTING YOU?"

A Prayer Spoken in Fear and Awe

As he was traveling, it happened that he was approaching Damascus, and suddenly a light from heaven flashed around him; and he fell to the ground and heard a voice saying to him, "Saul, Saul, why are you persecuting Me?" And he said, "Who are You, Lord?" And He said, "I am Jesus whom you are persecuting, but get up and enter the city, and it will be told you what you must do." The men who traveled with him stood speechless, hearing the voice but seeing no one.

ACTS 9:3–7 NASB

When Jesus asks the question "Who do you believe I am?" we better have a good answer ready. Saul obviously didn't have the right answer on hand.

He was a man with a mission, and his mission was to crush this new Christian faith. Why? He probably believed it was blasphemy and a threat to the peace. But if it was blasphemy, then it couldn't be true. Perhaps he believed Jesus was a con man or in league with the devil. Whatever idea he had about Jesus, it was fixed in his head and directed his violent actions.

But Jesus wasn't going to let Saul's murderous intentions get in the way of His plans. All He had to do was show up and tell Saul what He wanted him to do. No matter how set in his ways Saul was, the majesty and power of a personal appearance by the Lord was going to change his mind. Change his mind, blind him, blow him off his horse. . .

So Saul found himself in the presence of this spectacular being. He had the good sense to be humble and address the being as Lord. And, in a time that supposedly had many gods, he showed his ignorance of Jesus and also his lack of faith in his own idea of God by asking, "Who are you?"

Then Jesus let Saul in on the secret, telling him, "I am not who you thought I was—but I am the one you decided to stand up against. Now here's what I want you to do."

In the face of such a powerful reality check, Saul, an educated man, was wise enough not to object or complain that it couldn't be possible.

The impossible tales he had heard about this man were suddenly very possible.

The True Nature of the Word

The nature and identity of Jesus has been a subject for debate from the early days of the church. Some wondered if He had always known His divinity. Others speculated that divinity came upon him at a certain age. The notion of the Triune God, the three-in-one, took a while to arrive at.

Not surprising, really. Defining God must surely be a difficult matter.

Even in His lifetime, people debated His true identity—some thinking He was John the Baptist, some declaring He was the prophet Elijah. Apparently it was easier for people to believe dead men would walk among them than it was to believe God would do the same.

Jesus even asked His disciples, "Who do you say that I am?" And Peter gave the unequivocal answer, "You are the Messiah." In other words, the promised one, the Savior.

Each of us has to answer the same question if our journey in faith is to mean anything, and we do well not to be distracted by fads and notions, by deep-sounding philosophies or intellectual rebuttals.

We ought to start off humbly, like Paul in his enforced humility, and ask Jesus who He is. You will find, if you have an open heart, that He is the one your soul recognizes, the one it longs for. Start from there. It's not a long walk from that point to understanding that the home we miss isn't of this world and that Jesus has come to rescue us and take us there.

He died that we might go home.

So while we are here in this temporary accommodation, if He wants to take us out of our way and put us to some particular use, we ought to follow Saul's example once again, praying and going where He leads. The journey will only increase our knowledge of who Jesus really is.

The Answer to Saul's Prayer

Four words spoken in fear might not seem like much of a prayer, but Saul was talking to God in the form of an ascended Jesus. Talking to God is prayer whether it happens in a church or on a dusty road somewhere.

As for the answer—Jesus told Saul, there and then, who He was and what He wanted. Saul didn't even begin to quibble or question. He allowed himself to be led into the city like a little lost child, and once there, he spent the next three days fasting and praying.

Then began the less-than-easy task of integrating him into the group of believers. Not only had he recently been hunting them down, but he had a very different experience of Jesus than they did.

We can only wonder if Jesus' instruction to love their enemy took on a new depth at that moment.

167

The rest of the answer to Saul's prayer can be found in the Bible. In fact, it makes up a sizable chunk of the Bible. The letters of Paul (as Saul became) have been answering people's questions about who Jesus is ever since.

Practical Prayers

- Who are You, Lord? I think back to life without You, and I understand that You are my all in all.

- The Alpha and the Omega, the Father and You are one; nothing was created that was not created through You. The Bible tells us who You are on a grand scale. On a smaller scale, I am glad to also know You, Lord, as the lover of my soul.

- This side of heaven, dear Savior, I cannot presume to fully understand who and what You are, but I thank You for the opportunity to spend my life—and forever after—finding out.

42

"DEAR GOD, I DESERVE ANGER. BUT SOFTEN THEIR HEARTS, WILL YOU?"

A Prayer for a Family Reunited

Then Jacob prayed, "O God of my father Abraham, God of my father Isaac, Lord, you who said to me, 'Go back to your country and your relatives, and I will make you prosper,' I am unworthy of all the kindness and faithfulness you have shown your servant. I had only my staff when I crossed this Jordan, but now I have become two camps. Save me, I pray, from the hand of my brother Esau, for I am afraid he will come and attack me, and also the mothers with their children."

GENESIS 32:9–11 NIV

If the prodigal son had done well for himself and then wanted to come home, he might have understood Jacob's trepidation.

He hadn't distinguished himself as a son or as a brother when he had lived at home. In fact, he had conned his father and cheated his brother, aided and abetted by a mother who wanted her favorite son to have the best.

But since he had been away, he had—by necessity—done a lot of maturing. He was no longer the boy who dressed as his brother to convince a blind and dying father to give him his brother's blessing. He had been the victim of a con man himself, and he knew how it felt. He had also had to work hard—twice as hard as he ought to—to win the woman he loved as a bride.

But despite the changes in him, he knew the wrongs he had done as a younger man had gone unanswered for. He imagined the hurts he had caused had festered, unattended all the many years he had been away.

His trip home from the land of his father-in-law, Laban, wasn't exactly voluntary. The older man's behavior wasn't conducive to family harmony, just as Jacob's behavior had caused division earlier with his own family.

He was returning home a very wealthy man by the standards of the day, and he ought to have expected a hero's welcome. But he knew he hadn't departed a hero. And he knew his brother knew it too.

He sent messengers ahead, and those messengers told Jacob his brother was coming to meet him—with four hundred men! He feared the worst and asked God's protection from what he expected to be the justified wrath of Esau.

The Damage Done and the Damage Repaired

We live. We grow. (If we live right!)

The things we did as youngsters, or as unbelievers, don't go away just because we mature in life and in faith. Sure, we would do them differently now. But we did them wrong back then. Perhaps those incidents also helped shape the person we became, even if they only provided painful examples of what happens when we do wrong.

We aren't time travelers—we can't fix things by traveling back in time and not doing them. But we very often have to fix them. Sometimes we can make restitution for a loss we caused. Sometimes we can help someone we hindered. Often we simply set ourselves free from a nagging guilt and enable our journey to continue.

Jacob saw nothing wrong in the way he behaved to Esau—until someone else did something similar to him. Feeling the sting of being deceived, he understood better how his brother had felt. He grew beyond that kind of behavior but must always have imagined his brother was still stuck with the consequences of his actions.

So he prayed for protection. A more mature prayer might have been for forgiveness or for his brother to have prospered. Perhaps the night-long struggle before the brothers met was a further step in the maturing process.

God did protect him. He had done it a long time before by removing the bitterness from Esau's heart and leaving only the love.

It might do us all some good to look back over the path we traveled along and ask what damage we did on the way, then pray for God's help to put it right.

The Answer to Jacob's Prayer

Jacob prayed—but he was still afraid and took some precautions of his own. He sent his servants out as an advance guard with gifts of goats for Esau and the promise of his brother's love and loyalty. In this way, he hoped to placate his brother's anger.

Then, after nightfall, Jacob sent his wife, children, and all his possessions across the river into his brother's land. But he stayed behind.

Then one of the strangest events in the Bible took place. Jacob started wrestling with what seemed to be another man. The two wrestled the whole night. Then, as dawn was breaking and the other man realized he could not overpower Jacob, he touched his hip and dislocated it. But still Jacob would not let go. And, weirdly, he insisted on a blessing before releasing the other man.

The man renamed Jacob as Israel because, apparently, he had struggled with God and man and overcome. Despite the man refusing to name himself, Jacob declared he had seen God face-to-face. Despite the man saying Jacob/Israel had overcome, Jacob declared that his life had been spared.

The incident may be difficult to relate to the situation or the prayer, but it made a difference in Jacob as he then went out in front of his tribe to meet his brother.

His brother, Esau, against all expectations, ran to him, hugged him, and cried with happiness at seeing him again.

Practical Prayers

- Help me, oh Lord, to pray in full expectation of Your answer and not to preempt it on my own.

- Dear God, the thrust of my life with You must be forward, but if I might help someone who has stalled on the road—or who I might have knocked off the road—then may I, with Your wisdom and guidance, look back.

- The person I am now, Almighty God, is not the person I was then. Help me have mercy on the old me, as You did, and enable me to willingly and happily put right the things I broke in the past.

43

"ALMIGHTY GOD, YOU TELL ME THINGS MY MIND CAN'T COMPREHEND!"

A Prayer to Understand the Words of God

And I heard, but I understood not: then said I, O my Lord, what shall be the end of these things? And he said, Go thy way, Daniel: for the words are closed up and sealed till the time of the end. Many shall be purified, and made white, and tried; but the wicked shall do wickedly: and none of the wicked shall understand; but the wise shall understand.

DANIEL 12:8–10 KJV

Daniel is perhaps most famous for being thrown in the lions' den and not getting eaten. But as an end-times prophet, he gives John of Patmos a run for his money.

As a high-born Jew (and perhaps still a teenager), he was given special status when the Babylonians swept Israel and Judah off the map. Rather than being kept in slavery, he was allowed to live in the king's palace. He was still a captive and would remain one all his life, but he found freedom in his faith despite the pagan culture of the court.

The first half of the book of Daniel tells of how he and his friends stayed true to their God despite threats and actual attempts to make them pay for it with their lives.

As Daniel grew, his faith and steadfastness made him a trusted adviser at court, and when the king had problems his gods couldn't help with, he turned to the God of Daniel.

Standing on the bank of the river Tigris one day, Daniel received a vision. His companions saw nothing but were so terrified that they ran away. Daniel passed out and fell on his face in the dirt.

Despite this, the vision continues and a glorious man bids Daniel rise. This "man" reassures Daniel and then lays out a history of the future for him. At first, the future seems pretty much like the past with kingdoms at war and empires rising and falling, but then comes the time of the great Prince Michael and the realm of heavenly warfare, and Daniel was reassured that his people—everyone whose name was written in the book—would be delivered.

He was instructed to lock the words of the vision away until the end times, but was told that many would go to them to increase their knowledge.

Perhaps understandably, Daniel was confused. He said to the "man" (who surely had to be the Son of God), "O, my Lord, what shall be the end of these things?"

The Answers Aren't Always the Answer

Children always ask, "Why?" And it's a good thing. Really!

And good parents try to give answers whenever they can.

But sometimes, because of safety or sheer business, the parent just needs the child to do something without having to get it all explained to them. In an ideal situation, the parent says something, trusting the child will do it, and the child does what the parent wants, trusting it will be explained at some other time.

Now imagine you were running the universe! How much time would you have for explanations?

It's a feeble analogy, but trust is a big aspect of faith. Faith would be almost pointless without it. If we knew how everything was going to work out, then not only would we take it for granted but we might even argue against it.

So God tells us what to do (if we listen). We don't always understand, but we do it anyway and, surprise surprise, it works out for the best!

Of course, there are times—many times—when we don't get to see the results of what we do. Daniel didn't. Sometimes the results aren't for us or anyone we know. Sometimes we are simply an anonymous reply to someone else's prayer.

Would it make any difference to how you followed God's lead if you knew the ultimate benefit was going to be for someone else?

I didn't think so.

The joy of doing God's work doesn't lie in the answers or conclusions; it lies in simply knowing you are doing God's work.

The Answer to Daniel's Prayer

The shining man (let's just call Him Jesus) replied by telling Daniel to go about his business. No explanation would be forthcoming until the proper time. Daniel was to record His words for the education of the wise. Who they were or in what situation they might read those words he didn't need to know.

We are also told that Jesus was busy with other things. Imagine that. So this was a fleeting but important visit. Daniel had been selected to hear this message since he first declared his faith. Now he had heard it, and Jesus had to go.

A big element of faith is trust. It's only human to want to know the answers, but it isn't always divine to give them (at the time we want them).

Jesus gave the required information to the right man in the certain knowledge that it would be recorded and used as He intended. Explanations would take care of themselves, just perhaps not in Daniel's lifetime.

Still, Jesus did have time to reassure this man of faith, Daniel, that at the end of his days he would rise and receive his allotted inheritance. Perhaps with that inheritance, understanding would also come.

Practical Prayers

- Almighty God, let's face it. . .I'm not an almighty god. If You gave me all the answers I thought I wanted, it would spin my head off my shoulders. I am satisfied to know what You are satisfied to tell.

- Dear Lord, the answers to my life, my actions, are all around me. Give me eyes to see them and the wisdom to decipher them only so I might live a better life for You.

- Father God, I thank You for the words in the Bible that are beyond my understanding. Just like much of what I didn't understand as a child is now obvious to me, so I know Your Word will open to me at the right time. Amen!

44

"LORD, I SHOULDN'T BE ASKING YOU—BUT SAVE MY DAUGHTER!"

A Prayer for the Life of a Child

And when Jesus had crossed again in the boat to the other side, a great crowd gathered about him, and he was beside the sea. Then came one of the rulers of the synagogue, Jairus by name, and seeing him, he fell at his feet and implored him earnestly, saying, "My little daughter is at the point of death. Come and lay your hands on her, so that she may be made well and live." And he went with him. And a great crowd followed him and thronged about him.

MARK 5:21–24 ESV

Jesus was attracting big crowds. A string of miracles and healings meant that a large crowd followed Him just to see what He was going to do next.

This was a time when those of the established religious system ought to have had nothing to do with Him other than to look on disapprovingly.

Jairus was very much a part of the established system. He was one of the rulers of the local synagogue. Associating with Jesus might have cost him respect, position, and income, which is why the Pharisees who sought Jesus out for private talks did so at night.

No doubt Jairus cared about those things. After all, body and soul had to be kept together, he had a family to support, and no doubt he thought the role he played filled an important need for the local community. He cared—but he cared more for his daughter.

Love won out over pride. He was a father who believed his young daughter was dying, and that possibility tore at his heart. Doubtless he had already made the required offerings and said the proper prayers. She was still dying. The established system couldn't help—but this potential usurper might be able to. So in front of crowds of people who would have known him as a powerful man, Jairus fell at Jesus' feet and prayed for His help.

Jesus didn't hesitate in going with him. But He was delayed along the way by a woman who needed healing. As He spoke to the woman, commending her on her faith and telling her she was healed, a messenger arrived from Jairus's house, telling him there was no need to bother the teacher anymore—the little girl was dead.

Healing someone else's daughter had, apparently, kept the Lord from saving Jairus' daughter.

This prayer, it would seem, never had a chance to be answered.

What's Your Treasure?

How much did the things of this world—his position of influence, his income, his reputation, perhaps even his home—matter to Jairus as his daughter lay dying? Even in a society where child mortality rates would have been high and female children were not as prized as males, Jairus discovered that his daughter was worth more to him than all of these things.

Because, make no mistake, if Jesus had snubbed him or been unable to grant his prayer, Jairus would have been finished in the local community.

Love won over pride. Heaven won over the earth.

It often takes extreme times or examples like this for us to fully understand our real priorities.

A wise man or woman gives some thought to them and adjusts their lives accordingly before the extreme times kick in.

Jesus addressed this issue when He told us not to concern ourselves with building up treasure on earth but to focus on treasure in heaven.

It helps if we take some time to identify the aspects of our life heaven would approve of. Once we identify them, then we need to build on them. A father's love for his child would certainly be on the list.

As for the other stuff, the earthly stuff, well. . .we can't avoid it, but we can avoid being trapped by it. Imagine if Jairus hadn't been able to set himself free from his position as ruler of a synagogue.

The Answer to Jairus' Prayer

The messenger thought it was too late. The crowd probably thought it was too late. The whole world, had it known, would have declared it was too late.

Jesus looked at Jairus and said, "Don't be afraid; just believe" (Mark 5:36 NIV).

If ever there was a time when faith in Jesus was going to transcend the so-called real world, this would have to be it.

Jairus took Jesus to his home. Saying it like that ignores the possibility that he might have wept and wailed and refused to move; he might have blamed Jesus for being too slow and a fraud, anyway; he might have reacted a number of ways—but he took Jesus to his home.

Jesus assures the wailing mourners that the little girl is simply asleep and, despite their belief that the dead were asleep in God until the resurrection, they laughed at Him.

Then He "performed" one of His most amazing miracles in the most unostentatious of ways. He held her hand and said, "Little girl. . .get up!" (Mark 5:41 NIV).

And she got up.

Then Jesus suggested they get her something to eat. Coming back from the dead, as simple as He made it seem, obviously works up an appetite!

Practical Prayers

- Dear Lord, what You don't give me I don't need. Now I just need to remember that when the other side offers me the world and all the junk in it. You know. You've been there. And You set the example I want to follow.

- Treasure! The world would have us believe it is glittery, shiny, spendable stuff. Oh, what a con! Real treasure, God, comes from You. And You are love. Love may not be glittery and shiny, and it certainly isn't spendable—but it sure is heavenly.

- Pride is a trap, a weapon used against us. Dear Lord, I would count every time I broke out of that trap and lay in the dirt at Your feet a victory!

45

"FATHER, THIS MAN HAS BEEN CLOSED DOWN. OPEN HIM UP."

A Prayer for Speech and Hearing

And they brought to him a man who was deaf and had a speech impediment, and they begged him to lay his hand on him. And taking him aside from the crowd privately, he put his fingers into his ears, and after spitting touched his tongue. And looking up to heaven, he sighed and said to him, "Ephphatha," that is, "Be opened."

MARK 7:32–34 ESV

We have five God-given senses and we rely on them. Take any two of them away and we will be in difficulty. Take away hearing and speech, and we will be seriously disadvantaged. This man lived in a world without hearing aids and speech therapy, and where such infirmities were often seen as punishment for sin.

Perhaps the man could hardly speak because he had been deaf from birth and had never heard speech, or perhaps it was a physical problem. We have to hope his family and friends had some method of communicating with him, even if only to tell him who they were taking him to see. And we ought not to ignore the faith of "some people," probably people who loved the man, who took him to Jesus for healing.

The simplicity of the Lord's response is worth noting. He didn't question anyone, He didn't hesitate or say He was too busy—He simply took the man aside to a quiet place. He spat, He touched the man's ears and tongue—actions almost too commonplace to mention—and then He raised His eyes to heaven.

It is one of the distinctions of Mark's Gospel that the actual words Jesus spoke are often recorded as He said them. So, we know Jesus said "*Ephphatha*," which means "be opened" or "open up."

The crowds watching must have been regularly disappointed by Jesus' lack of showmanship—but they could hardly ever have been disappointed by the results.

What Good Might We Do?

Two common themes ran through most of Jesus' miracles (and His life): prayer and simplicity. Unlike the witches, magicians, and wonder-workers of His day, He never put on a show. He simply got the job done—and gave credit where it was due.

A wise man (or woman) once postulated the question, "What good might you do—if you didn't care who got the credit?" We might reword that to read, "What good might we do—if we were content for God to get all the credit?"

The way to do that is to trust that God directs your steps and whatever is put in front of you is there for you to help or to learn from. The way not to do it is to see the situation in front of you and tell yourself it is someone else's business and you are only there coincidentally.

Jesus didn't set up shop and wait for people to come to Him. He went about His mission and helped or healed people as the Father brought them to Him.

And He used whatever He had on hand, remembering that the world was created and thus holy.

A little spit on His hands gave hearing. A little mud on His finger gave sight. We might not be quite at that level of competence, but we can be of use, even if only by using our ears to listen or our voice to speak words of comfort and life.

The Answer to Jesus' Prayer

Well. . .guess what? The man who was deaf and could hardly speak was given the gifts of hearing and speech.

Knowing about Jesus and the Bible stories as most people do, this is hardly a surprise anymore. But imagine what it would have seemed like if you had been standing there watching it happen. Or if it happened to you!

We don't know what happened to the man after that, but being able to speak clearly for the first time, no doubt he spent a lot of time talking about the man who made that possible. Perhaps he became a disciple, perhaps he became another living example of Christ's work. Perhaps he went away and lived an ordinary and fulfilled life. That too would have been a gift greater than he could have expected.

The people who saw this prayer answered were impressed. They said, "He has done all things well. He even makes the deaf hear and the mute speak" (Mark 7:37 ESV).

Could it be they were thinking of the time Moses protested that he wasn't a good speaker and God asked him, "Who gave human beings their mouths? Who makes them deaf or mute? Who gives them sight or makes them blind? Is it not I, the LORD?" (Exodus 4:11 NIV).

To those who knew their scripture, the identity of the one who answered this prayer must have been obvious.

Practical Prayers

- Almighty God, the enemy would close us down in so many ways, not just through our senses. He would close down our hopes and our hearts and our lives. I pray to You to keep me open in every way that is essential for faith, love, and life.

- Dear Lord, help me to keep it simple, to offer love in whatever situation You might choose to place me. And all glory to You.

- How can I help? So often the question has stopped me from helping. May my question, and prayer, from this day on be, "How would You have me help?" Amen!

46

"GOD, YOU CAN TAKE AWAY MY AFFLICTION. BUT YOU WON'T."

A Prayer for Ease of Pain

So to keep me from becoming conceited because of the surpassing greatness of the revelations, a thorn was given me in the flesh, a messenger of Satan to harass me, to keep me from becoming conceited. Three times I pleaded with the Lord about this, that it should leave me.

2 Corinthians 12:7–8 esv

Peter never let the fact that Jesus said he would be the rock His church was built upon go to his head. Perhaps because he remembered well his humble and foolish beginning as a headstrong fisherman.

But Paul might have had good cause to think his mission was greater than even that of Peter's. And he had started out as a privileged youth and a powerful man. Thinking himself important might never have been a big intellectual leap for him. But he didn't take it.

And here he explains why.

It seems the church at Corinth had been swayed by other versions of the Gospel taught to them by more glamorous and exciting "super-apostles." Paul pleaded with them to put up with his plain old foolishness for a while, and he recounted his history in faith and the things he had suffered for the gospel. He was embarrassed to do it, but he did it for their sake. The plain truth was as close as he would come to boasting about himself like the "super-apostles."

When laid out simply, it made a very impressive résumé. He had been a persecutor of Christians; he met the risen Christ in person and was tasked with teaching the gospel to the Gentiles; for His sake he had been flogged, stoned, beaten with iron rods, imprisoned, shipwrecked, starved, frozen, and faced persecution from the Jews, the Gentiles, and the Romans. But still he kept going when another man might have given up.

Was that not impressive? Was that not something he should be very proud of?

For another man. . .yes!

But Jesus didn't have any time for proud men. And He must have seen a likelihood of it in Paul's character. So He afflicted him with an impediment Paul refers to as a "messenger of Satan."

Despite repeated prayers, this "thorn" in Paul's side was never removed.

There's Strength in Being Weak

Nobody's perfect. And, given the example of the people who think they are perfect, we ought to be grateful for that.

Hurt people know how to comfort, people who have known loss know the importance of giving, only those who have sinned can fully understand forgiveness and give it in the spirit it is meant to be given.

In a very counterintuitive way, it is our weaknesses that make us strong, but only if you equate being forgiving, generous, and comforting as strong. The world doesn't usually. The world usually thinks of strong people being without any weakness and perfect people being devoid of flaws. Yet another way God's view of the world and the world's view of itself don't match up.

It might be strange to say that God delights in our weakness. But, let's face it, even the strongest of us is so very weak compared to Him. Perhaps the "weakness" we talk about here is nothing more or less than the realization of where we are in the relationship.

The ones who think they run the show or are in control of their own lives. . .well, there's really no space for God there. If He wants to work with them, He really has to knock all their strong defenses down and have them start again. The "weak," in that respect, are the ones who willingly allow Him in.

Accept your imperfections. Don't be proud of them. But let God make beautiful things out of them.

The Answer to Paul's Prayer

The answer to Paul's prayer was no, no, and no again.

You can almost imagine God shaking His head and thinking, "Take a hint, Paul. It's there for a reason."

The phrase "thorn in the flesh" was certainly a metaphor and is never properly explained. Perhaps the fact that Paul didn't explain it implies that it was all too obvious to his audience—a physical defect of some kind. Some translations of the Bible do record it as a painful physical ailment.

Another option, more in keeping with the "messenger of Satan" theme, is that Paul was haunted by his past and the things he had done. It might have been difficult to think of himself as too wonderful when a certain degree of shame was always with him.

Obviously it was something neither Paul nor the medical experts at the time could fix. He knew God could undo it, but he also believed God had caused it to keep him humble, and the negative answer to his three prayers seemed to reinforce that. Remember, Paul was a man used to conversing with the Lord. He knew a deliberate silence when he heard one.

The message must have gotten through to the Corinthians as they kept his letter and it became part of the church canon. So his unanswered prayer helped answer his prayer that the church in Corinth stay faithful.

Practical Prayers

- Dear Lord, I understand that whatever my physical short-comings are, You do not judge me by them. You love my soul. If anything, You see those shortcomings as something for me to grow through, or something that enables me to get alongside the ones You want me to help.

- Pride! I can't grow a flower, I can't raise the sun, I can't make rain or hold planets in their orbits, or heal a cut, cause nails to grow, make a kitten, build a whale, or change the seasons. But I can be proud of the one who does all that and so much more.

- Super-apostles of one type or another abound even today, Lord. Help me look beyond the flash and the razzle-dazzle and the style to the heart and the deeds and the love of Your Word.

47

"I DIDN'T RECOGNIZE YOU, LORD! WHAT CAN I DO FOR YOU?"

A Prayer for God's Will

And it came to pass, when Joshua was by Jericho, that he lifted up his eyes and looked, and, behold, there stood a man over against him with his sword drawn in his hand: and Joshua went unto him, and said unto him, Art thou for us, or for our adversaries? And he said, Nay; but as captain of the host of the LORD am I now come. And Joshua fell on his face to the earth, and did worship, and said unto him, What saith my Lord unto his servant?

JOSHUA 5:13–14 KJV

This wasn't a conventional prayer. And Joshua wasn't a conventional man. He had graduated from a servant of Moses to one of the greatest war leaders Israel had ever known.

His life was dedicated to God's will, but the book of this capable man is lacking in prayers. Perhaps his vision was so clearly defined he rarely had to ask for help.

But when God's messenger appeared before him, he didn't hesitate to ask what the Lord had in mind. As prayers go, "I'm listening" is a particularly useful one.

Joshua stayed true to the example of Moses as he prepared to lead the Israelites into the Promised Land. He had the people consecrate themselves in the morning and promised the Lord would do amazing things. Having made that promise, even he wasn't prepared for all that happened.

The ark of the covenant was sent on ahead, and it caused the river Jordan to dry up, allowing the Israelites free passage. Then, in preparation for battle, Joshua had all the men born since the Exodus circumcised. The people ate of the produce of the land—and the manna stopped coming. It seemed they were absolutely where God wanted them to be.

And then they faced the first major obstacle to their occupation of the Promised Land—the fortified city of Jericho!

Joshua had sent spies to scout the city, and he knew the inhabitants were terrified by the prospect of battle, but the walls were thick and the gates were firmly shut. The Israelites, after forty years wandering in the desert, were unlikely to have siege weapons.

As he pondered these things, Joshua saw a man with a sword standing between him and the city. He asked the man whose side he was on, and the man said, in effect, "Neither! I am on God's side."

Having met face to face with the commander of heaven's armies, Joshua did the only possible thing. He threw himself in the dirt and asked what God wanted him to do.

Nay, I Will Not See You as an Enemy

"Art thou for us, or for our adversaries? And he said, Nay!"

There's a witty one liner that says, "You know you have made God in your image when He hates the same people you hate." Of course, those of us who do that present it a little differently, insisting God hated those people first.

It's a trap we have to avoid, though. And this episode from the book of Joshua reminds us of it.

The man with the sword is disdainful of the idea that he might be on one side or another in an earthly battle. He is on God's side.

Abraham Lincoln is supposed to have echoed that idea when he said, "My concern is not whether God is on our side; my greatest concern is to be on God's side."

God doesn't hate our enemies because we hate them, or even because they are in the wrong. He isn't concerned with our squabbles. He is too busy looking into the heart of each man and woman regardless of their side. What He sees there will determine His relationship with them, regardless of our opinion of them.

Perhaps we could try and follow that example—looking past the differences of politics, nationality, the football team they support, or the nasty thing they said the other day, and looking instead at their hopes, their fears, their loves and losses. And try to see them as God does.

The Answer to Joshua's Prayer

It was a time of wonders, and Joshua had seen many of them. He doesn't seem to have flinched when the commander of the hosts of heaven told him he would bring down the walls of Jericho with trumpets, shouts—and the ark of the covenant.

The Israelites, their priests, and trumpeters marched around the city walls carrying the ark for seven days. The tension in the city must have built up to an unbearable level. On the seventh day, as the trumpets blew, the previously silent army gave out a roar. And the walls of Jericho came tumbling down.

A great many impossible things became possible when the ark of the covenant was with you. And God's blessing.

The Israelites, who had been warned to spare the household of Rahab, the woman who had helped their spies, and to leave the devoted things of the city untouched, swarmed into Jericho. Perhaps in the excitement of the battle it was too much to expect them to remember two instructions. Rahab and her family were spared, but the Israelites had a checkered past when it came to holy objects. Nothing much would change on that score for a long time.

But Joshua had asked, listened, and seen the incredible reply to his prayer played out in front of him.

Practical Prayers

- Our Father in heaven, when I pray, remind me not to say "What?" when You answer in some wonderful way I couldn't possibly imagine working out. Let me just go with it, prepared to be amazed again!

- Dear Lord, I understand You would have none of us as enemies and instead all of us gathered together as Your children. And that isn't going to happen if I run around treating people as enemies. Sorry.

- The ark of the covenant was a mighty weapon because Your Word dwelled in it. I understand that with You dwelling in me, I too can be a mighty weapon. Give me the power to bring down walls—walls of division and hatred. And may I be a force for unity in Your name, Jesus. Amen!

48

"MAY GOD TAKE YOU BACK."

A Prayer for Restoration

And Araunah looked, and saw the king and his servants coming on toward him: and Araunah went out, and bowed himself before the king on his face upon the ground. And Araunah said, Wherefore is my lord the king come to his servant? And David said, To buy the threshingfloor of thee, to build an altar unto the LORD, that the plague may be stayed from the people. And Araunah said unto David, Let my lord the king take and offer up what seemeth good unto him: behold, here be oxen for burnt sacrifice, and threshing instruments and other instruments of the oxen for wood. All these things did Araunah, as a king, give unto the king. And Araunah said unto the king, The LORD thy God accept thee.

2 SAMUEL 24:20–23 KJV

Angels! They aren't much like the winged dolls we set on our Christmas trees or the golden pins we wear on our jackets.

They are messengers of the Almighty. As such, they usually convey His words and intentions, but they can also be the conduits of His power and wrath.

God was angry with Israel and Judah, not for the first or the last time. So He gave King David a choice of punishments. None of them pleasant.

On behalf of the people, David had to choose between three years of famine, three months of fleeing from their enemies, or three days of plague. Greatly distressed, David decided it would be better to be at the mercy of the Lord than the country's enemies.

So an angel was sent to unleash a plague, and seventy thousand people died. When the angel reached out a hand to destroy Jerusalem (Really! Just by reaching out a hand!), the Lord had pity on them and stopped the destruction. The angel had reached the threshing floor of a man called Araunah the Jebusite.

David was horrified! He took full responsibility and asked that any further punishment fall on him and his house.

God did not respond to David directly. Instead He sent Gad the seer to tell David to build an altar on the threshing floor when His wrath had been overtaken by His mercy. The fact that God was now using an intermediary to talk to him must have been extremely upsetting for the king. He would no doubt remember that God had talked to him through Nathan when he had Uriah killed.

Araunah, who must have been aware of what was happening, offered David the threshing floor and all the equipment in and around it as a gift. Then Araunah, who is known for only this incident, added something beautiful to his offering—the prayer that David's God would accept him again.

Take All I Have, and One More Thing

There are times when people get into trouble and it is entirely their fault. We might wonder if they will simply go on to do the same things again. Or we might feel justified in walking on by, hoping they learn from the experience.

But sometimes people fall out, lash out, or get hurt, and they aren't at all sure why. Life, love, and the spiritual battles of this world can be complicated. In this instance David sinned, and God was suddenly, horribly, against him.

Understanding David needed to build an altar, Araunah offered to give him everything he needed and added a prayer of reconciliation into the mix. There was nothing in this for Araunah. In fact, it would have cost him a great deal. But he would have helped right a wrong situation. He would have helped restore a loving relationship.

When we see situations of hurt and confusion, it can be tempting to stay a safe distance away, lest we get entangled. But if we can build a bridge there, by a practical offering of help or by prayer, we really ought to.

Hurt, confusion, and broken relationship serve only the enemy. Love restored is to the glory of God. It might cost you time and effort but, as Araunah surely found, what you are really buying is treasure in heaven.

The Answer to Araunah's Prayer

David declined the offer of Araunah's workplace for free, insisting that any altar he built he should pay for, otherwise he was short-changing God. But he could hardly refuse the prayer. It would have been his heartfelt desire as well.

David bought the threshing floor, made the altar, and gave offerings of fellowship. God halted the plague.

We can be reassured that David's God accepted him once again. Despite a turbulent relationship, David was known as a man after God's own heart. David's last words were in praise of the Lord, asking, in effect, "Is not my house right with God? Has he not made with me an everlasting covenant?"

God would include His own Son in the lineage of David. Jesus is often referred to as the "Son of David." What greater honor could He bestow?

This may have been the Lord's plan all along and may have had little to do with the prayer of a miller. But every prayer counts, and at a pivotal and upsetting time, Araunah's kindness may just have warmed the Lord's heart toward King David.

Practical Prayers

- Almighty God, there can be nothing sadder than a person estranged from You. Sadly, it happens all too often. If I may be a bridge between You and a wayward child of Yours, then I will willingly lay myself down.

- Dear Lord, King David gives me hope. He tried and failed and tried again. If ever I find myself adrift from You as he was, and confused as to how to find my way back as he was, please send me an Araunah.

- Possessions don't come into it. Rank and profession aren't important. All that matters is our relationship with You. May I guard my own relationship and help others with theirs, whatever the cost.

49

"A BABY, LORD? BUT HOW CAN THAT BE?"

A Prayer That God's Will Be Done

And Mary said to the angel, "How will this be, since I am a virgin?" And the angel answered her, "The Holy Spirit will come upon you, and the power of the Most High will overshadow you; therefore the child to be born will be called holy—the Son of God. And behold, your relative Elizabeth in her old age has also conceived a son, and this is the sixth month with her who was called barren. For nothing will be impossible with God." And Mary said, "Behold, I am the servant of the Lord; let it be to me according to your word." And the angel departed from her.

LUKE 1:34–38 ESV

God was about to do a new thing!

In the Old Testament, He had given children to Manoah's wife, who was barren and older, and Sarah, who was well past the usual childbearing age. In the New Testament, He repeated the miracle with Elizabeth, who would become the mother of John the Baptist.

But each of these women had a husband in their lives.

The baby He had in mind to send this time was a little different. It was none other than His own Son—Himself in human form. So there could be no doubt who the father was, He chose a young woman who had never lain with a man.

Hardly anything is recorded about Mary's early life. Some have speculated she was dedicated to the temple as a child. But Luke makes it clear that she was a young woman living in Nazareth and pledged to be married to a man named Joseph. Joseph was of the house of David and Mary may have been also. So, long after the life of the great king, the house of David was a large one and justifiably proud of their lineage.

But Joseph and Mary would have been nothing special in their hometown. He was either a carpenter or a construction worker and was considerably older than his bride-to-be.

Their life was rolling along, much in the style of their neighbors, but a plan and promise made long ago was about to be implemented. They may have known the prophecy, but would never have imagined it might come into the world through them.

We don't know what Mary was doing when Gabriel, the Lord's messenger, appeared to her, but we know his words—that she was highly favored—troubled her greatly. That would surely have to be an understatement.

Gabriel explained God's plan—that she would bear the Son of the Most High.

Young as she might have been, Mary knew where babies came from, and she wondered how this was to be brought about when she had never lain with a man.

She asked, but she didn't say it was impossible. And she didn't run away.

Mission Impossible. Choose to Accept It

Sure, it's impossible. But you must not have been paying attention if you think that's a problem.

Both Mary and Joseph would have known the Old Testament stories, just like we know the Bible. But there's a difference between knowing them and having one step into your life.

How we handle that difference speaks about our faith. If we read about God and His miracles and what He asks of his people every Sunday and then refuse to believe it when something similar happens on a Tuesday morning or Friday afternoon, then our faith could probably do with some work.

Miracles of God were absent from Israel for a long period between the Old and New Testaments. Mary might not have known of any happening in her lifetime. But when one happened to her, the only question she had was the fairly sensible one of "How?" The explanation she received probably didn't enlighten her all that much. But she accepted that God would work it out and she would be a part of it.

People have achieved lesser miracles by stepping out in faith. They feel called to do some work for God, and they have no idea how it can possibly happen. So they step out in faith, and then watch in wonder as God makes it happen.

Forget the whole idea of impossible. If God wants you to do something, feel free to ask how—but don't let that stop you from walking forward to find out.

The Answer to Mary's Prayer

Gabriel explained to Mary what was going to happen, and that she would not be alone in this. Elizabeth, a relative of Mary's, was already traveling down a similar path.

Elizabeth and Mary would be a great comfort to each other, and Elizabeth's unborn baby would jump in recognition of Mary's unborn baby.

If there was ever any question over the wisdom of choosing a simple country girl for such a monumental mission, Mary put it to rest with her response.

Despite a woman's status and future security being dependent on her purity and her husband's faithfulness, Mary, who was only engaged (or promised) at the time, said, "I am the Lord's servant. May it be to me as you have said."

In those few words, Mary risked her earthly future and guaranteed her heavenly one.

Joseph was, of course, confused and upset by this turn of events. He thought about sending his bride-to-be away to spare her dignity. But Gabriel spoke with him. And Gabriel's words are God's words. Joseph understood that.

The end result of Mary's prayer—her questioning, her listening, and her acceptance—was that Jesus Christ, the Savior of humankind, came into this world in the most humble but the most loving of circumstances. And we were saved because of it.

Practical Prayers

- I understand, Lord, that I may never fully understand what You have in mind for me. And You understand that I will be confused and ask questions from time to time. It's how we move beyond that that matters—You unfolding Your complex and wonderful plan, and me walking in trust.

- You tell me You are going to do something I know to be impossible. I am laughing, Lord, because why would I expect anything less of You? Let's show the world that everything is possible in You.

- "May it be to me as You have said." May Mary's prayer always be my prayer. You gave me this body, Lord, and You will call it home when You are ready. Until then, I'm trusting You will put it to good use in Your awesome plan.

50
"FATHER, FORGIVE THEM; FOR THEY KNOW NOT WHAT THEY DO."

A Prayer for All Humanity

And when they were come to the place, which is called Calvary, there they crucified him, and the malefactors, one on the right hand, and the other on the left. Then said Jesus, Father, forgive them; for they know not what they do. And they parted his raiment, and cast lots. And the people stood beholding. And the rulers also with them derided him, saying, He saved others; let him save himself, if he be Christ, the chosen of God.

LUKE 23:33–35 KJV

This is the prayer that changed everything!

We take God's forgiveness for granted these days, but the fact that Jesus even uttered this prayer suggests it might not have been a foregone conclusion. If it was, then why waste a dying breath on it?

At first glance, this seems like one of the strangest prayers in the Bible. God is talking to God here. How can that be? Well, without getting into the metaphysics of the Trinity, Jesus was God, but He was also a man. Hence the doubts, the fears, the need to find time to talk to "Himself."

Which one of them spoke these words (if such a separation is even conceivable) we will never know in this life. We just ought to be thankful they were spoken.

Jesus had completed His ministry. He had proclaimed the kingdom of God and, with some notable exceptions, the world hadn't listened. Not only did the earthly powers not listen, they wanted Him permanently out of the way, so they brutally murdered Him.

Look back through your Bible. God had struck people down for lesser offenses. Now they were killing His Son. Jesus' intercession at that moment was either nothing much, just some throwaway words, or they changed things forever.

The people in the world who most needed to hear His message truly didn't understand. They didn't understand they were being kept in the dark—their actions, lives, and souls were being twisted by an enemy they couldn't see. There was no human justification for what they did to Jesus. What they didn't understand was that Satan was pulling their strings. Jesus asked that they—we—not be held automatically accountable for that.

He wasn't asking that they be forgiven for the lashing, for the metal spikes driven through His hands and feet. He was begging we be forgiven for our blindness.

So we might be led into the light.

Make Heaven Where You Are

Let's be honest. It either was the hardest thing you ever had to do—or it's something you haven't yet found the ability to do.

Forgiveness!

People make it out as a soft thing, a sign of weakness. But many powerful people can't bring themselves to forgive a hurt. They make excuses, like saying it's for fools or weaklings, but they physically couldn't force themselves to do it.

Now, your situation may be as dramatic as that, or it may not, but it still isn't easy. Ask yourself this. What would happen if you forgave that person? I don't mean let them take advantage of you in any way, but simply forgave them. Can you think of bad stuff that might happen as a result? No? Might good things come about because of it? Emotional, tearful, life-affirming things? Yeah?

So ask yourself what force keeps you away from that. Who wins if you stay unforgiving? And do you want to be on their side?

Or do you want to be on the side of a power that has the capability to radically change the world and may only be waiting for you to help?

The Answer to Jesus' Prayer

The soldiers were not struck down!

It seems a little thing, but it marked the beginning of a new covenant with God.

The fact that everything changed was felt by the earth itself. The sky darkened, the ground quaked. We are told that holy men rose from their tombs and walked the streets of Jerusalem.

What? How much of God's love must have come into the world at that moment to reanimate those who had dedicated their lives to Him?

The accounts are confusing and varied and seem to make little sense—which makes them more real. If someone made up a story like this, it would hang together better. The fact is that everything changed in a way mortal minds couldn't begin to understand. So they wrote down the best they could that *something* had happened.

The temple veil was torn, but Jesus also tore the veil from our eyes. Now that we could see the battle that was being fought, we were forgiven our ignorance. We could choose which side we were on. And we could choose our way out at the end—through Him.

But it doesn't end there. Jesus, who dying in this world asked that we be forgiven, will also stand by our side in the next life, asking the same.

In the face of such love, how can we not believe? In the face of such forgiveness, how can we not accept?

Practical Prayers

- Jesus, lover of my soul, You died for me. And as You died, You forgave me. The one I can't forgive hurt me, deceived me, hurt those I loved, and none of that compares with what You went through or what Your forgiveness gained for me. Perspective. . .I really need to work on that!

- They cannot see—or I cannot see! Very few set out to hurt for no reason. For most it happens through ignorance, thoughtlessness, or because of hurts they have suffered. Lord, they might not see the damage they do, but with Your help, I might see the damage that caused them to hurt. And with just a little of Your strength, I might forgive.

- Uttering words of forgiveness, dear Lord, You set Yourself free from this world. Bitterness, resentment, and anger are very real earthly traps. Uttering words of forgiveness, may I follow Your example and set myself free.

FOREVER AND EVER, AMEN

"For Thine is the Kingdom, the Power, and the Glory. Forever and ever. Amen."

The Doxology traditionally ends the Lord's Prayer. Perhaps surprisingly, the earliest versions of the Gospels don't have it. The words of praise were added by the early Christian churches and have been used to end the Lord's Prayer ever since.

The word that ends this ending will also be used to end other prayers, and to express emphasis or to show willingness. When the preacher says something particularly profound someone will usually shout out "A-men!" The most tender, whispered prayer will end with the same word.

We say *amen* in different situations without wondering at the slightly different meanings. But don't worry, all the meanings are good ones.

Amen usually means "so be it." It is either a way of accepting that God's will *will* be done, or a plea that it might work out the way we need it to.

Another meaning is "truth" or "it is true."

Before Jesus, people used it as an affirmation of something someone else had just said, proclaiming it to be the truth. Jesus used the word a little differently. Where He says, "Verily, I say unto you" (in the KJV) the word He used instead of the Old English term "verily" was "Amen." In using it at the beginning of the statement, He was letting it be known that He was not affirming anyone else's words. He was stating His own truth.

Perhaps not surprising from someone who is "the way, the truth, and the life" (John 14:6 KJV).

In the book of Revelation, He is actually referred to as "the Amen" (3:14 KJV).

We may sometimes use the word casually, concentrating on the content of the prayer rather than the ending. We might use it to agree with someone or call it out in excitement, but there is no bad way to say amen.

It is a little word with some big, powerful meanings. We use it to end our prayers, so what better way to end this collection of prayers?

Whether our prayers are pleas or thanks, whether we are supporting our preacher or restating a biblical truth, may we always remember that Jesus is the truth. He is our Amen.

If we give our troubles to Him in prayer, He has the power to change our lives for the better. And *that's* the truth.

Amen?

Amen!

SCRIPTURE INDEX